PRAISE FOR PAUL FERRINI'S BOOKS

"Paul Ferrini's writing will inspire you to greater insights
and understandings, to more clarity and a greater resolve to make
changes in your life that can truly change the world."
NEALE DONALD WALSCH

"Paul Ferrini is a modern-day Kahlil Gibran—
poet, mystic, visionary, teller of truth."
LARRY DOSSEY, M.D.

"Paul Ferrini is an important teacher in the new millennium."
— IYANLA VANZANT

"Paul Ferrini's work is a must-read for all people who
are ready to take responsibility for their own healing."
JOHN BRADSHAW

"The most important books I have read. I study them like a bible!"
ELISABETH KÜBLER-ROSS, M.D.

"Paul Ferrini reconnects us to the Spirit Within, to that place where
even our deepest wounds can be healed."
JOAN BORYSENKO, PH.D.

"I feel that this work comes from a continuous friendship with the
deepest part of the Self. I trust its wisdom."
COLEMAN BARKS.

"Paul Ferrini's wonderful books show a way to walk lightly
with joy on planet earth."
GERALD JAMPOLSKY,

Book Design by Paul Ferrini
and Lisa Carta

Library of Congress Control Number
2007923621

ISBN # 978-1-879159-69-3

Heartways Press
9 Phillips Street, Greenfield MA 01301
www.heartwayspress.com

Manufactured in the United States of America

A COURSE IN SPIRITUAL MASTERY PART SIX

EMBRACING
Our True Self

A New Paradigm Approach to Healing our Wounds,

Finding our Gifts, and Fulfilling our Spiritual Purpose

PAUL FERRINI

TABLE OF CONTENTS

Author's Preface

Three years ago, I thought that my work was done. I had written over thirty books on love, healing and forgiveness and I had led transformational workshops and retreats all over the world. But my guidance indicated that there was still more for me to do. Human pain on the planet was intensifying and there was a need to create a transformational process that would enable people to heal their wounds and step into their roles as facilitators and leaders in the new millennium.

Over the last three years our Spiritual Mastery Process has helped numerous individuals heal their wounds and change the beliefs that keep their self-betrayal in place. You will read some of their stories in this book. These courageous individuals were able to face their deepest and darkest fears, heal their childhood traumas, and step into their power and purpose as authentic human beings. Each learned to take off his mask and become real to himself and others. Each learned to find her gift and step forward to serve others.

I know that these stories will inspire you to commit to your own healing process. Indeed, that is why I wrote this book. And that is why my students are willing to share these very personal and revealing stories with you. They know that if healing is possible for them it is possible for you too.

This book presents a new paradigm for the healing journey that integrates the insights of depth psychology and spirituality.

This new paradigm approach recognizes the necessity of healing of our deep childhood wounds as a prerequisite for understanding who we are and what we have come into this life to do. It makes it clear that we cannot meet our True Self until we heal our trauma, correct our erroneous beliefs about ourselves, and dissolve our reactive behavior patterns.

Our healing process helps us realize that in order to meet our True Self, our False Self must die. This ego death experience creates a psychological and spiritual crisis in our lives in which we are asked to surrender our ego agenda and meet our fear head on. It invites us to get in touch with our core wound and heal our shame and unworthiness.

To grow, we must go through this crisis. We have no choice. The old ways of living no longer work for us. We know we have to stop allowing fear to run our lives. We know we have to stop betraying ourselves. We can no longer live the life that others want for us. We can no longer live out of sacrifice or guilt. We have to let go of all that. We have to risk being ourselves, regardless of how scary a proposition that is.

This book provides a roadmap and a guide for weathering this spiritual crisis. It presents real life stories of people who have healed their wounds, discovered their gifts, and learned to live in harmony with their spiritual purpose. If you are looking to meet and honor yourself at the deepest level, read these stories with an open heart and an open mind. They will recall you to your truth and help you to manifest it.

Many years ago, my teacher told me "I am the door to love without conditions. When you walk through, you will be the door." It took a few years for me to see just how powerful these words were.

Three years ago, I invited my readers to come and experience directly how "to love without conditions." Many came and tested the waters. A few stayed and learned at depth. They learned to embody the energy of unconditional love and acceptance. They walked through the door just as I had walked through many years before.

Now they are able to hold the door open for you. They are the living proof that Spiritual Mastery is not some abstract, far off goal, but a living process that is accessible to all who are willing to do the deep work.

This book holds the door open for you. I invite you to walk through it.

Paul Ferrini

PART 1

Meeting Ourselves

The Core Self cannot be wounded.
That is because it is whole and complete.
There is nothing lacking in it,
nothing in it that needs to be fixed.

The Core Self

The Core Self is our essence. It is who we are at the most fundamental level. It is the connection point between our divine origin and our human incarnation. It is the divine spark that we bring with us into this embodiment. It includes all the gifts and talents we possess in their potential. It is what makes us unique. It is the blueprint we are born with.

All of us have a Core Self, but not many of us are in touch with it. That is because the Core Self can be encountered only with unconditional love and acceptance. If we look without love and acceptance, we will not see the Core Self. We will see the wounded self. The wounded self grows up with conditional love and lives in a state of fear. It seeks love but cannot find it.

The Core Self cannot be wounded. That is because it is whole and complete. There is nothing lacking in it. There is nothing in it that needs to be changed or fixed.

When we are connected to our Core Self, we are connected to all that is. We live in relationship to our Source or higher power. We abide in who we are.

The Core Self is our energetic connection to Love. It connects us heart to heart to each other. When we rest in the Core Self, there is no separation. There are no separate bodies or separate agendas. There is just infinite, boundless love.

When we abide in the Core Self, we are incapable of judgment. We cannot trespass or defend. We cannot find fault. We know that we are loveable and acceptable just the way that we are and so are others.

Our Core Self is the resting place of Universal Love. It lives there, breathes there, and moves out from there into the world.

The Core Self has been called Tao, Atman, Christ, Buddha nature, and so forth. It has many names and is spoken of in many traditions. We call it the "Core Self" because it is the essence and the center of our Being.

The Core Self is eternal, consistent, unchangeable. In this sense, it is not subject to the ups and downs of physical existence. Some say it is not born and does not die because it exists beyond the vicissitudes of this world.

The Core Self is there, even though we have not encountered it. It cannot be destroyed or taken away from us. However, it can be disguised, covered over or ignored. And it can take some of us a very long time to remove those disguises and come face to face with our essence.

THE WOUNDED SELF

The Core Self is overshadowed by the wounded self. That is because we see everything through our pain. Indeed, the shadow is sometimes so dark that we don't see the light behind it.

How do we know we are wounded? We know because we have pain or distress of some kind. We are triggered in our relationships. We have reactive behavior. We fight with others or run away from them.

We know that we are wounded because there is a lot of fear that comes up and we don't know how to hold that fear compassionately. We don't know how to be with our fear or the fear of others.

We know that we are wounded because things happen that make us very angry at ourselves or at others. We feel overwhelmed by feelings of grief, jealousy, unworthiness.

We know that we are wounded because we can't find peace in our hearts or in our relationships. In addition, we may have memories of a traumatic event that altered our life such as rape, incest, the death of a parent or another experience of abuse or abandonment.

ARE OUR WOUNDS REAL?

The wounded self is not ultimately real, but it feels very real to us. We believe that this is who we are. We identify with our wounds. We feel shame and guilt. We feel pain and unworthiness. We feel less than or more than others. We attack, defend, build walls between self and other. We push away love because it does not feel safe. We hurt ourselves or we hurt others. We shame ourselves or blame others. We abandon those we love or they abandon us. We live inside a vicious cycle of attack and defense. No matter how painful it is, we don't seem to be able to stop it. We don't know how to stop being a victim or a victimizer. This is the psychological world most of us inhabit, individually and collectively.

Shame and victimhood operate on many levels. Some are more obvious than others.

WHY ARE WE WOUNDED?

The wound helps us to know who we are. It creates awareness. When we are wounded, we are challenged to understand something about ourselves and others.

Before we experience the wound, we are totally connected with all that is. There is just Oneness. Spirit, God, call it what you will. There is no division, no dark or light, male or female, high or low, good or bad. There is no differentiation or comparison. Oneness does not allow for growth in consciousness. It is already the alpha and the omega, the beginning and the end.

But as soon as you have two of anything—two people or two flowers—you have differentiation and the basis for comparison and judgment. You have dark and light, self and other, human and divine. You have the opposites. What we know of the world is created out of this inherent duality.

The wound itself comes from this duality. It is experienced as soon as we lose our consciousness of oneness. As such, it represents our fall from grace and our entrance into the world in a human body.

So how do we experience the wound here in the body in the world? We may have been created as equals, but we do not feel that we are equals, nor do we treat each other as equals. We feel "less than" or "more than." We compare, judge, attack and defend. Wounding is a very real affair in our human world.

People strike out at us because they themselves are hurt or afraid. They abandon us for the same reason. Sometimes we are abandoned and there is no reason. That brings a different kind of pain.

There is no child who is not wounded by his parents. And there is no adult who does not carry deep, unhealed childhood wounds.

If we want to feel "one" with ourselves, with each other, or with our Source, we must learn to forgive ourselves and our brothers and sisters for the inevitable wounding that happens here on planet earth.

Why are we wounded? What is the purpose of the wound? What is the reason for suffering? These are important questions.

The wound enables us to obtain knowledge of Self, to know the part of God that is us. Once we know the part of God that we are, we can see the God-Self in others.

The wound is a tool of consciousness. It creates separation and with it understanding of oneness. How can you understand what oneness means if you have never felt separate?

The wound causes us to believe that we exist as separate entities, that we are born, that we suffer and that we die. Yet, as we learn to heal the wound, we discover the truth about ourselves and each other. We discover that there is a Core Self within us that is beyond birth and death.

But that comes much later, after we have investigated the wound and healed it.

THE SHOCK OF SEPARATION

We all need to get in touch with the shock of our separation from Source. As soon as the light of consciousness comes, the darkness comes with it.

We have pain. We feel separate. We want to run and hide. Or we want to attack back.

The wound is the beginning of the division of the psyche from one into two, from oneness into duality.

In the beginning, there is only the undifferentiated, dark oneness of the Mother's Womb. Freud called it the oceanic experience. All babies come into the world through this womb. It is the transition space from one realm to another, from unmanifest to manifest, from darkness to light.

Even in this birthing experience, there is discomfort in utero. There is birth trauma. There is wounding.

The baby screams when he enters the world. The umbilical cord is cut, separating him from the mother. His eyes open and he is shocked by the light. He is no longer shielded and protected from the world by the mother's womb.

As a little baby, he experiences many pains and struggles. He is hungry, his tummy hurts and the breast or the bottle is not always nearby. He goes to the bathroom and his diaper is wet and uncomfortable. There are loud noises and unanticipated falls.

The wounding has begun and there is no way to escape it. If he has a loving mommy or daddy, his pain is mitigated. If not, his pain intensifies.

Millions of babies are abused, neglected or abandoned. Some are beaten or sexually abused as soon as they learn to walk. I do not have to tell you this story. You know it well. If it did not happen to you, it probably happened to someone you know.

The world is a harsh place to be. Things happen to us that overwhelm and terrify us. We learn to shut down emotionally. We learn to stuff our pain. We don't want to feel it. Indeed, sometimes our pain is so great that we truly believe that feeling it would completely destroy us.

This is the beginning of the division within our psyche. It is inevitable.

THE MASK THAT HIDES OUR PAIN

We are all wounded, but we do not easily acknowledge the pain that we are carrying. Just as the Core Self is overshadowed by the wounded self, the wounded self is covered over by our persona.

We pretend to be happy when we are not. We pretend to be confident when we are terrified. We learn to wear a mask that hides our fear, our shame, and our pain. We think that wearing the mask will bring us love and acceptance, but it does not. It just moves us further and further away from our essence.

Some of us learn to contrive very sophisticated masks. They fit around us so tightly we can hardly breathe. It is not until we collapse on the street that we realize the extent of our self-betrayal.

No matter how good the mask, it eventually cracks or wears thin. Denial cannot last forever. Eventually, our wound begins to bleed through. The disguise no longer works. That is the time when most of us fall apart. In the best case, we have an emotional breakdown and end up in a mental hospital for a week or two. In the worst case, we overdose on drugs or try to put a bullet through our head.

It isn't easy to admit that we have failed to live behind our mask. What we don't realize is that everyone fails. All masks fall away. The wound can and must reveal itself. We cannot heal our wounds until we stop denying them.

It seems strange that some of us would rather die than admit how much we hurt. But that is how deep our shame is. And that is how hard it is to tell the truth when we live in a culture of denial.

REMOVING THE DOUBLE CLOAK

So here's the rub. Until we acknowledge our pain and take the mask off, we cannot encounter our wound. And until we encounter and heal our wound, we cannot find our Core Self.

To meet the Core Self, we must go through an emotional healing process in which we feel our pain and acknowledge and forgive the wound. That enables us to reclaim our innocence.

When we reclaim our innocence, we come face to face with our Core Self in all its shining beauty. For the Core Self is innocent and unstained. It is completely whole and intact.

It cannot be wounded.

As long as we condemn ourselves or others, we cannot meet the Core Self. In order to meet the Core Self, we must forgive all our trespasses against others and all their trespasses against us. In order to meet the Core Self, we must heal our wounds.

That is the nature of the healing journey. And that process of healing and forgiveness is the subject of this book.

THE FALSE SELF

Before the mask rips and our world falls apart, we can be quite content living behind our disguises. Many of us develop a very elaborate mask that involves adult roles and responsibilities. It seems that we are living a successful, well-adjusted life when in truth we are not living the life we want to live. We are living to please others. We are doing what we think that we are supposed to do. We are living a lie. We are not honoring the unique being that we are.

The False Self no doubt has many masks and roles. Indeed, it probably has a different disguise for each occasion. The False Self represents all the ways in which we have learned to betray ourselves in the search for approval. It is our attempt to find love and purpose outside of ourselves. Needless to say, it is a futile attempt. It does not work.

It is only a matter of time before the False Self begins to destruct. Holes appear in its armor. Long denied emotions like grief or rage erupt. The outer skin—once perfectly made up—becomes wrinkled and blemished. The hair—once neatly cut and permed—becomes ragged and disheveled. One just cannot hold the False Self together any more. Like humpty dumpty, our outer persona falls off the wall and shatters into hundreds of pieces.

It simply cannot be put back together again. But this death leads to an important rebirth. From the ashes of the False Self, the True Self is born.

THE TRUE SELF

The birth of the True Self is often called a Spiritual Awakening experience. It is not always a pleasant experience, because the old self that betrayed us must die for the new self that honors us to be born.

The False Self with its ego agenda and search for happiness outside of itself must come to an end. The shamed-based search for love and approval must be abandoned.

We must throw away our mask and with it the need to disguise or deny our pain. We must have the courage to look our fear, our shame, and our hurt. We must go willingly into the darkness of our psyche to reclaim the light. In the process we will encounter our unworthiness and learn to transform it.

Many spiritual students try to skip over this step on their journey, but it does not work. Lest we heal our wounds, we cannot encounter the Core Self. In the end, we will simply give our power away to some other person or idea.

Real healing happens when we have the courage to go where we hurt most. We must go through the tunnel of our pain to see the light that lies beyond it.

If we are courageous enough, we will find the roots of our pain and unhappiness. We will forgive ourselves for the pain we have caused and forgive others for hurting us.

We will wipe the slate clean and start life on a new page. That is when we come face to face with our Core Self. That is when we discover who we are and who we have always been. That is when we give ourselves permission to step into our purpose and manifest the blueprint of our incarnation.

CORE SELF AND TRUE SELF

The Core Self is always there, but we do not meet the True Self until the False Self dies. Another way of saying this is "We *are* the Core Self. We *become* the True Self."

When the False Self runs our life, we don't know or see the Core Self. But when the False Self is shattered, we see who we really are and we decide to honor that.

The False Self betrays the Core Self. The True Self honors the Core Self.

The Core Self is not really of this world. It is of the heavenly realm. It is in our heart of hearts. It in our essence.

The True Self is the expression of the Core Self in the world. It is in the world, but not of the world.

All of our talents and gifts exist as potential in the Core Self. They are developed and expressed by our True Self. The True Self is the engine of our creative expression.

Because it is aligned with the Core Self, the True Self is energy incarnate. It harnesses the kundalini energy and puts it to work in our lives.

The Core Self is a noun, an essence, a potential. The True Self is a verb. It is action, movement, fulfillment.

The Core Self is nurtured by Divine Mother. Her work is all about helping us love and accept ourselves just the way we are.

The Truth Self is the empowered by Divine Father. His work is all about helping us discover and express our creative gifts.

These two aspects of our Spiritual Nature work together. We need both the masculine and feminine aspects of our divinity. We need to learn to receive love so that we are able to give it.

23

None of us have parents who love us or empower us unconditionally. That would be too much to expect, for they are wounded like us. We are the only ones who can show up to mother and father ourselves in this way. That re-parenting process is essential to our healing work. To do it, we need the help of both Divine Mother and Divine Father.

BEING AND DOING

The Core Self is about Being. The True Self is about Doing.

For most of our life, our False Self has been attempting to manifest our soul's purpose, but it could not do it. Only the True Self can do that.

When we try to create or express without encountering our essence, all we create is the wound. Every attempt to do without being is simply wrong doing. It leads to wrong relationship, wrong livelihood. It merely fuels the collective wound and its seemingly endless cycle of violence and inequality.

None of this shifts until we come face to face with the Core Self. When we meet the Core Self, we align with it, and everything we do is congruent with it. As a result, we spontaneously honor self and other. This leads to right action, right livelihood, right relationship.

All doing must dissolve into being. There it finds its purpose. Then it can go forth and act in alignment with that purpose. This is how we learn to live in harmony with who we are.

PART 2

Healing the Divided Psyche

Neither shadow nor persona
is an accurate representation of who we are.
They are both distortions of self
because each conveys only part of us.

Only when the two are integrated
and the psyche returns to wholeness do we begin
to get a realistic sense of who we are.

Shadow and Persona

Because we stuff our pain, part of our experience and the emotions associated with it is repressed and locked away. The psyche is split in two. The part that we don't want to see or feel is called the Shadow and the part that we accept is called The Persona.

The shadow includes the early childhood experiences that were too traumatic for us to process consciously. It includes all our fears and demons that run our lives at an unconscious level.

The Persona is that aspect of self that we are comfortable with and allow others to see. We keep developing our Persona in order to win the acceptance and approval that we want from others. We believe if we make ourselves "lovable" we will receive love.

Those who like our persona become our friends. Those who don't become our enemies.

The Persona is a mask or a disguise that we wear in an attempt to hide our pain and our shame. We believe that if we can hide our pain, then people will find us more attractive, worthy, and loveable. The mask, however, is a lie. It is a pretense, a sham. Wearing the mask is our attempt to be something we are not. It is inauthentic and essentially dishonest. It says to other people "I'm cool. I don't hurt." when in fact we are feeling the pain of our wound.

It is hard to find the person behind the mask unless the mask comes off. In the beginning, most relationships between people are really relationships between their masks. But it is only a matter of time before the mask rips or wears thin and the person behind the mask reveals him or herself. Generally, it isn't a pretty sight.

Behind everyone's mask is pain, fear, anger, shame, grief, envy, you name it. Behind the mask is a wounded being. That is true not just for some of us. It is true for all of us.

Each of us has both a shadow and a persona. The shadow is the "bad" or "dark" side of us. The persona is the "good" or "bright" side of us. Actually, neither shadow nor persona is an accurate representation of who we are. They are both exaggerations or distortions of self because each conveys only part of us. Only when the two are integrated and the psyche returns to wholeness do we begin to get a realistic sense of who we are.

THE WOUNDED CHILD

The Wounded Child is another name for the shadow. Sometimes it is easier to personify the shadow as a child because the shadow self is fairly simple, primitive and unsophisticated. It is selfish, scared, angry, demanding, and is prone to throwing temper tantrums. It thinks of itself as bad and feels unworthy of love. It is just like a hurt little kid.

We were all hurt little kids once, so we can relate to this. Many of us have had children and we can recognize the hurt little kids in them.

It is easier to approach the hurt part of ourselves if we see it as a child because we know that no matter how much a child acts out all he really wants is love. Actually, that is what the shadow wants too. It wants love and acceptance. And it created a persona to try to obtain them. Unfortunately, the mask was not effective. How could it be? What was created in fear cannot bring love.

Those who are attracted to our mask, usually flee from us when the mask comes down. The best they can offer us is temporary, conditional love. When they see the angry, sad, wounded face behind the mask, they abandon us and our pain just deepens.

No. The Mask does not deliver. It cannot bring the love it was fashioned to bring. So in the end, the mask be cast away. In the end, we realize that love cannot come from the outside. It has to come from within.

WOUNDED BELIEFS AND BEHAVIORS

The wounded child internalizes certain erroneous beliefs about itself. These beliefs are the operating system of its computer and all of its programming runs on that operating system

Most of these beliefs stem from our shame and unworthiness. They all say in one way or another "I am unworthy of love." For example, one belief might be "I'm stupid." Another might be "I'm ugly."

The behavior resulting from these beliefs will either be confirmatory or compensational. In other words, we will either try to manifest that belief or we will try to prove that it is wrong.

For example, if I believe that I am fat, I will either become fat or I will do everything that I can to be thin, regardless of the cost. I will wear a mask of thinness. I may even become anorexic or bulimic in the search for love and acceptance.

If I believe that I am stupid, I may sit at the back of the classroom and try to be invisible (confirmatory behavior) or I might sit in the front row, participate aggressively and try to win the teacher's approval (compensational behavior). I may even take this compulsive behavior into adulthood, becoming a chronic underachiever or overachiever. In the former case, I may have trouble going to school or keeping a job. In the latter case, I may earn one PhD after another and build multiple businesses in the attempt to prove that I am worthy of love.

We either manifest our core belief or we find a way to hide it. We either wear our hurt on our sleeve or we build a mask to cover up the inadequacies we perceive in ourselves.

All masks need to come off if we want to heal. Each of us must take the time to feel our pain and see our self-betrayal. We cannot change our behavior without seeing the belief on which it is based. And we cannot challenge that belief without seeing the shame and unworthiness behind it.

NOT BELIEVING OUR OWN LIES

All of us cling to our mask because we believe that if people really knew the rage, the grief, the fear, the guilt, and the shame that we carry within, they would reject us. We learn to stuff our emotional wounds into the dark depths of the psyche where we assume no one will go looking.

We do such a good job pretending, we even begin to believe our own lies. We look at our lives through our mask and see no wounds there. We have a great home, a great spouse, a great job, great kids, and money in the bank. Who could ask for more?

An elaborate, tightly constructed mask is bound to work for a while. It may stay in tact for a year, for five years or for twenty years. Sooner or later, however, the mask begins to crack.

Sooner or later, some Pandora comes along and opens the black box hidden in the depths of our psyche. Maybe someone close to us dies, we get into an auto accident or we start a tempestuous relationship that pushes our buttons and brings up our childhood wounds.

Once the black box has been opened, all the ghosts and goblins come tumbling out. Jeckyll meets Hyde. Humpty Dumpty comes off the wall and shatters into thousands of pieces. The False Self crumbles. The mask rips and betrays the tortured face of the child, ranting and railing.

The schizophrenic divide, the iron wall that stands between persona and shadow is finally compromised. Through the holes in the wall our pain can be seen and heard.

We can no longer be in denial. We can no longer pretend to be happy and intact. Our brokenness has come to light. Our wound has been revealed.

I have often said that I have met only two types of people in this life: people who are aware of their pain and people who are in denial about it. But I have never met anyone who has not been in pain at one time or another in his or her life.

Denial is not a river in Egypt or, if it is, it is a long, circuitous one. It takes a lifetime to navigate it. Rather than taking that detour from the heartland into the head, we can save ourselves a lot of time by going into the root of our pain and dealing with it.

Those who deal heal. Those who don't deal don't heal. End of story. Your healing cannot begin until you drop your mask. Are you willing to take it off and allow yourself to be authentic? Are you willing to be imperfect, vulnerable, human?

If so, healing can begin. If not, better turn back now. This journey of transformation will require of you all of this, and more.

THE WALL BEHIND THE MASK

When we take off our masks, we meet our pain head-on. Unless, of course, we are an addict. If we are an addict, we try to compensate for the pain, or distract ourselves from it, by seeking some kind of pleasure (food, drink, drugs, sex, etc), but that "fix" works only temporarily. And then we need more of our substance of choice to "fix" our pain and we need it more frequently.

In this way, our addiction becomes the issue. No matter how hard we try to hide it, our addiction eventually results in highly conspicuous, self-destructive behavior. Our lives become increasingly dysfunctional and begin to fall apart. Our addiction becomes a call for help.

Thanks to 12 Step programs, help with addictions is within the reach of most people. But ending the addiction is only the first step in recovery. True recovery means not only "not using," but coming face to face with the pain behind the addiction. It was this pain that the addict tried to escape by using. Now that he is not using, he has to come face to face with his pain or he will not heal the cause of his addiction.

Addiction is a wall that we build between ourselves and our pain. When we recover from our addiction, we have to learn to take down that wall. If we don't, we will recover from our addiction, but we will not recover from our pain. True healing will not be possible for us.

Let us remember that addiction is only one form of denial of our pain. There are many others. We can bury ourselves in work, making money, watching television, or surfing the Internet.

Anything that takes us up into our heads and away from our hearts can be a tool of denial. We can find new addictions or compulsive activities to replace the old ones. If we don't want to feel our pain, we won't. We will leave the wall standing and keep our pain locked away behind the wall.

The severity of our addiction forced us to take our mask off. Let us not find a new one to wear. Recovery itself can be a mask that we wear to keep our pain hidden and at bay.

If we want to heal fully, we have to resist the tendency to build a new mask. We have to be willing to stand there naked, vulnerable, visible, without a mask. Then we can begin to dismantle the wall and look at our pain.

Acknowledging our pain and looking at it is the first step forward on our journey of healing.

MEETING OUR PAIN

Once we stop trying to avoid our pain, we can begin to look into its causes. We can ask the question "Why do I hurt?"

The simple answer to this question is that we hurt because we have been wounded. Each one of us has many wounds. Some are superficial. Some are deep. Some are recent. Some go way back to our childhood or perhaps even in utero. In some cases, we may even be carrying ancestral wounds that go back to previous generations.

One way into our pain is to ask, "What hurts most right now?" For example, perhaps three months ago your marriage fell apart and your spouse moved out of the house. That's the recent wound. But behind that wound will be another. For instance, perhaps you married a critical woman like your mother. So not only are you experiencing the break up of your marriage, you are also experiencing your mommy wound.

Your oldest child may be acting out taking drugs and skipping school, rebelling against mommy just like you did when you were younger. The severity of your anger at him may surprise you until you realize that your son's actions are triggering your anger at yourself.

All our wounds can be traced back to a core wound. Understanding that core wound and your reaction to it is extremely important if you are going to heal your pain.

CORE WOUNDS

Our Core Wound usually results in some kind of shame or unwothiness. Here are some examples of Core Wounds.

- Abandonment (Physical and Emotional). Includes death or illness of parents or their unavailability because of divorce, active military service, addiction to drugs or alcohol, etc.

- Betrayal (Trust is established then betrayed). Includes ambivalence or emotional instability of caretakers including the mental or physical illness of parents

- Abuse (Physical, Emotional, Sexual, Ritual)

- Incest (Emotional, Sexual). Includes lack of appropriate boundaries or inappropriate behavior by parents, siblings or other family members

- Confinement, Imprisonment, Control

- Lack of Limits/Too much freedom

- Stolen Childhood/Caretaking of Parents or Siblings, being forced to take on adult responsibilities before we are ready

- Pampering, Spoiling, Low Expectations, Overprotection

- Danger/Lack of Safety (Physical or Emotional)

- Guilt, False Responsibility (for a parent or sibling's death or illness, etc)

- Birth Trauma, Birth Defects, Premature Birth

- Serious or Extensive Illness in Childhood

- Not being Wanted, Unplanned Pregnancy

- Rejection by a Parent, Post-Partum Depression of Mother

- Persecution by Siblings

- Repeated Humiliation, Criticism, Shaming, Blaming by Parents or Significant Others

The wound may be inflicted by Mommy, by Daddy, by a sibling, by another family member or by a significant other. Some wounds can be inflicted by a total stranger, or simply by life or fate.

There are Mother Wounds and Father Wounds. A Mommy Wound involves too much, too little, or inappropriate attention from Mommy. A Daddy Wound involves too much, too little, or inappropriate attention from Daddy.

Most of us have a Mommy Wound and a Daddy Wound. Often the Mommy and Daddy Wound run together as in the case where we have a critical, controlling mother and a weak or absent Father. In other words, too much Mommy often means too little Daddy and vice versa.

CORE BELIEFS

Our Core Belief about ourselves is created out of the shame or unworthiness attached to our Core Wound. Our Core Belief drives our experience of ourselves and the world. All core beliefs can be summed up by this one: "I am not worthy of love."

Here are some other examples of Core Beliefs:

- Nothing I do is good enough.

- I'm a bad or evil person (or I would not have been beaten/sexually abused).

- I am unworthy. I don't deserve to breathe the air.

- I am a failure. I will never amount to anything.

- I am stupid. Others are smarter than I am.

- I have to be smarter than others to be loved.

- I am unattractive.

- I am weak or sickly.

- I am unlikable, awkward, foolish, etc.

- I am unlovable.

- The world is not a safe place. If I am not careful, I will be hurt.

- I show up for others, but no one shows up for me.

- Love is too scary. I am better off alone.

- I can't do it by myself. I need someone to do it for me.

- I have to do it by myself. No one else can help.

- My needs do not matter. I have to take care of others (Mommy, Daddy, etc.).

- Whatever I do, it won't be enough.

- When I trust the universe, I get smashed.

- If I stand up for myself, I won't be loved.

Put a check mark next to all of the Core Beliefs listed above that belong to you. Underline the ones that are most important. If you do not see your Core Belief on the list above, please add it to the list.

Take some time to work on identifying your core wound and core beliefs. The healing process requires that you identify where you hurt the most and what beliefs lurk in your subconscious and run your life.

REACTIVE BEHAVIOR PATTERN

Our reactive behavior pattern is the way that we react when fear comes up. Some of us respond to fear by internalizing it (stuffing it) and some of us respond by externalizing it (projecting it onto others).

If we have an *Inward Reaction Pattern,* we try to hide from others or become invisible when we get scared. We become physically or emotionally inaccessible, self absorbed or obsessed. We run away or disappear. We don't confront others. We internalize our anger. We blame ourselves. We become a victim.

If we have an *Outward Reaction Pattern,* we attack others when fear comes up. Our behavior is emotionally or physically intrusive, aggressive, or overbearing. We are verbally or physically abusive. We yell, hit, blame and shame. We express our anger without owning it or looking at it. We become a victimizer.

Generally, we tend to copy the reactive behavior pattern of our dominant parent and to attract relationships with people who have the opposite behavior pattern, thus reliving the psychodynamics of our parents' relationship. We must become conscious of these dynamics and our part in them if we are going to change them. Otherwise, the dynamics will be reinforced and we will pass these patterns on to our children.

THE DOMINANT EMOTION

The dominant emotion is the way that you are feeling most of the time. Here are some examples of dominant emotions:

- Sad
- Angry
- Envious
- Hurt
- Anxious
- Fearful
- Worried
- Depressed
- Manic
- Depressed/Manic (up and down, big mood swings)
- Paranoid

Feel free to add to the list. Your dominant emotion will usually be quite obvious to others who are close to you. So if you don't know what it is, ask your spouse, your children, or your coworkers.

LOOKING INSIDE TOWARD THE WOUND

You dominant emotion is a symptom of something deeper that needs your awareness and attention. If you keep asking the question "Why am I depressed (angry, sad, etc)?" you will begin to peel back the skin of the onion and get closer to the core wound.

First, you uncover your reactive behavior pattern and see how it creates suffering in your life. You see how this pattern repeats itself in most of your key relationships.

You start by looking at your present relationships with spouse, children and coworkers and notice what triggers you in those relationships. Then you look at previous relationships, going all the way back to your relationship with your mother and father.

You see where the reactive behavior pattern originated.

You keep peeling back the onion until you discover your Core Belief about yourself and your Core Wound.

Then, after you get in touch with that wound, you look at the ways in which you covered up your hurt and your pain and sought to hide them from sight. You look at the persona you created in the attempt to obscure the shadowy material that scared or overwhelmed you.

You look at the False Self that you created in the search for love and acceptance and you see clearly that this False Self can never be happy. That is because the word that best describes the False Self is "betrayal." As soon as we construct a False Self, we betray our True Self.

Self-betrayal is the ultimate wound and all of us have it. Not only are we wounded by others, and that results in shame, but we have betrayed ourselves, and that results in even greater shame.

Of course, we did not betray ourselves willingly and consciously. We were under duress. We did the only thing that we knew how to do. We accepted conditional love. We twisted ourselves into a pretzel trying to please others and win their approval.

Of course, this does not work. We don't get the love that we want and self-betrayal has a very high cost. It leads to a variety of addictions/compulsions and self-destructive behaviors. In the end, the False Self shatters and we realize that we cannot pick up the pieces.

We need to start all over again, learning to honor and respect ourselves. This is what it means to be born again in this life. The old life that was a lie has to die. The mask must be buried. And the new, authentic life must be born.

This takes great emotional courage and honesty. Without it, emotional healing cannot happen, and spiritual transformation cannot begin.

THE HIDDEN JEWEL

The True Self is what is left behind when you take the False Self away. Drop the mask of denial and stop betraying yourself and you begin to discover who you really are. This does not happen over night. Just as it took a while to create the mask and invent the False Self, it takes a while to discover the True Self.

I like to see the True Self as a new, pristine continent to explore. It is virgin territory and there are no maps to guide you. You have to make the map as you go.

The agenda of parents and other authority figures drops

away. Now there is only your agenda, what you want for your-self, your experience, and the choices that you make each day. It is your journey and you must own it.

Of course, that means that you are responsible for the choices that you make. Welcome to real adulthood. As a child, you had excuses. Now you have none.

The life you have now is the one that you create. There is no one out there who is going to look over your shoulder, protect you, take care of you, or fix your mistakes. You are the architect of your own life. You are responsible for everything you create.

Most people don't want this kind of responsibility. That is why they never grow up. They remain wounded children. They hold onto their excuses. They would rather shame or blame others than take charge of their lives.

You cannot step up to this kind of responsibility until you have begun to heal your Core Wound. Your wound keeps you a victim or a victimizer. And, as we know, all victimizers were victims once.

The cycle of violence lurks inside each heart. That is why the healing of each person from his or her Core Wound is critical. There can be no collective healing of humankind until indi-viduals heal their wounds and end their self-betrayal.

The True Self in you is a shining jewel. There is a gift within the True Self that you have come here to give. Unless you find that gift and learn to give it, you will feel that you have wasted your time in this life. You will have lived without discovering and fulfilling your life purpose.

THE GIFT

When we begin to live in a way that is authentic, we start to get in touch with the unique gifts that we come into this life with. If we are lucky, these gifts are not a mystery to us; others have noticed them and encouraged us to develop them. If we are not lucky, others have failed to notice and we must discover our gifts from the inside out.

Your gift includes the talents and strengths that you have. You might have physical strength, dexterity or endurance. You might have emotional sensitivity, strong intuition, or compassion for others. You might have intellectual prowess, analytical ability, and problem solving skills. You might have listening skills, healing hands or the capacity to understand and interpret dreams.

There are as many gifts as there are people. Your gift is what you do well without great effort. It comes naturally to you. You enjoy cultivating and giving your gift and others appreciate receiving it.

Many people do not know what their gifts are because they have spent their lives listening to others. They might have tremendous artistic talent, but when the parent tells them "You can't be an artist because you will starve," they turn away from their talent and pursue something that is more acceptable to the parent or other authority figure.

That is why one cannot truly access the gift until one stops listening to others. The act of listening deeply to ourselves and honoring our desires leads naturally to the discovery of our gifts.

All of us come here with strengths and weaknesses. In our healing process, we learn to accept and accommodate our

43

weaknesses. Sometimes we even find ways to turn them into strengths. But unless we are masochistic, we find ways to work toward our strengths and away from our weaknesses. When we work toward our strengths, we discover our gifts and develop the confidence that we need to give them.

Self-betrayal often results in the attempt to do something that we don't have the talent for. As a result, it leads to failure and can demoralize us.

There comes a point for each one of us when we need to stop trying to shove a square peg into a round hole. When we engage in work that we experience as painful, difficult, or stressful, we can be sure that we are not working to our strengths. No good can come of this.

We must learn to defer to others who can do the job better than we can. Let us welcome those who have the strengths needed to accomplish the task at hand and be grateful for them. Their strengths will offset our weaknesses and vice versa. That is the key to creating any cooperative venture.

Admitting our weaknesses may be the first step that we take toward discovering our strengths. When we know what we are not good at and refrain from doing it, we make room for more appropriate work to come into our lives.

Many people tell me "I don't know how to honor myself."

"That's easy, " I tell them. "Stop betraying yourself and you will be honoring yourself."

The same people often say, "I don't know what I am supposed to do. I don't know what my purpose is." I tell them, "If you want to find your purpose, be clear on what your purpose isn't and refrain from pursuing that direction."

When you come to a cul-de-sac in your life—and self-betrayal is the ultimate cul-de-sac—you have to retrace your steps and see where you got off the main trail. Don't be afraid to admit your mistake. Don't push blindly ahead, hoping that you will come back on course. Turn around. Admit you were wrong.

You will not find your gift as long as you are trying to manifest someone else's gift. That does not work.

You won't find your gift outside of yourself or through the ideas and opinions of others. You have to look inside and keep your own counsel. The gift is there. Be patient. Listen deeply and you will find it.

If you have spent twenty years doing work that is not fulfilling, and you really want to discover your gift, you have to do a few important things:

- Stop doing what is not fulfilling.

- Start listening to your heart and honoring yourself in little ways.

- Be ready to try something new, especially if it feels right.

Don't let security concerns prevent you from taking a necessary risk in your life. Learn to trust yourself. Learn to surrender to the beauty and clarity of your own guidance. Connect with what is joyful to you and trust in that. What is joyful to you will also be joyful and inspiring for others.

Most of all, take little steps. The journey of a thousand miles begins with a single step.

Take that step now. Focus on the first mile. The other 999 miles will take care of themselves.

CONGRUENCE AND EMPOWERMENT

The True Self has its roots in the Core Self or the Spiritual Essence. When we lose touch with the Core Self, we cannot help but create a False Self. But when we are in touch with our Core Self, all that we do is congruent with It. The True Self is the embodiment or expression of the Core Self in the world.

We are the Core Self whether we are aware of it or not. We become the True Self. It is a choice. We put down what is false and accept what is true about us. Our ego – the architect of the False Self—dies or submits to a higher authority.

This is nothing less than a spiritual awakening. We can no longer betray ourselves. We have to be faithful to who we are. We have to be authentic and unique. When we make the choice to trust what is true within us, the True Self shines in all its glory. We become, as St. Francis did, an instrument of the Divine will.

Now all the chakras line up. Heaven comes to earth. Grace rules and miracles abound.

When the True Self is born, we come into our full empowerment. We are ready to find our gifts and to give them. We are ready to serve.

PART 3

Uncovering the Wound

*I spent thirteen years running all over the globe
trying to find happiness outside of myself.*

*It didn't work. In the end,
I had to come home and face my own fears.
I had to do the work my parents had never done.*

*I had to heal my wounds so that I could learn
to show up for myself and for my family.*

Dahlia's Story

If we really want to understand what makes us tick, we need to start exploring the roots of our pain and dysfunction. To do that, we must start at the surface and work inward. Here is an example.

Dahlia is a middle-aged woman who presents as timid, shy, and lacking in self-confidence. The words that seem to describe her overall state of being are "fearful and overwhelmed."

When Dahlia asks, "Why am I feeling fearful and over-whelmed?" the answer she gets is that the world is a scary place and she doesn't feel safe there. This is one of her core beliefs.

When she asks, "Why do I believe that the world is not a safe place for me?" she gets "That was the message that Mom gave to me. Mom told me that I had to be very careful. She overprotected me and so I did not make many mistakes or learn from my errors. As a result I did not develop resilience or gain confidence in myself."

Dahlia's mom did not let the little girl expand and trust her wings. Dahlia had to keep limiting herself so that Mom would be okay. She developed the mask of "the good little girl" who never really let her energy come out because that would upset mommy. Even as a teenager, she held back. She hardly dated at all and, even when she did, she was "little miss prim and proper."

Dahlia's mom told her that the most important thing in life was to find a husband who would adore her and take care of her. So that's exactly what Dahlia did. She married a man who was "safe" and had the financial ability to take care of her and her children.

What Dahlia did not know is that Mommy's fear tactics came from her own wound. When Mommy was seventeen, she was pretty wild. She fell in love with an older, married man and got pregnant by him. He told her that he was going to leave his wife and marry her. But he didn't. He abandoned her and she had to have that child all by herself. Not only that. Mommy's pregnancy wasn't something her Dad could easily accept. Even though he supported her and the child, Dahlia could always feel his judgment and resentment.

It seemed that Mommy was not attracted to stable men. She fell in love with men who brought out her wild side. They were daredevils who liked to take risks and have fun. They tended to be carefree and unstable. One day they had money and the next day the money was gone. Mommy chose men who were the opposite of her strict and overbearing father because she had a Daddy wound. Dahlia's father was one of those men.

But Mommy was going to make sure that things were different for Dahlia. She would make sure that Dahlia did not make the same mistake that she made. And, indeed, Dahlia did not. She continued to live inside her mask. She married the man that mommy wanted her to marry. Indeed, she lived out the life that mommy always wanted to have.

The problem is that it was mommy's life, not Dahlia's life.

When Dahlia came to her first retreat, she began to get in touch with the pain that she felt in her marriage. She had married a man she respected and admired, but didn't really love. He was the perfect provider and father to her children, but he did not meet her needs for intimacy.

Dahlia felt trapped. She wanted out of her marriage, but she refused to abandon her children. And she did not want to hurt her husband either, because he was a good man. But most importantly, Dahlia did not want to disappoint her mommy. She knew that if she told mommy she was thinking of leaving Rick, mommy would have a nervous breakdown.

All her life, Dahlia had been the perfect little girl and the dutiful daughter. This was her mask and her False Self. She believed deeply within her heart that she would lose mommy's love if the mask began to rip and she made a decision that mommy did not like.

Dahlia's core belief is "If I don't do what mommy needs me to do, mommy will not love me and I won't be safe. Bad things will happen to me."

The very idea of making a different choice than the one mommy wants her to make fills Dahlia with a ton of anticipated guilt. She just can't bear the idea of disappointing mommy. So she stays locked in her pain.

FINDING OUT WHERE IT HURTS

Gradually, Dahlia gets in touch with her present pain and follows it back to where it originates. She thinks her pain has to do with being trapped in a marriage about which she is conflicted and ambivalent. And yes, that's true. But what is the root of that pain? How did she get in this predicament?

Well, that's easy enough to see. She listened to mommy. She did not listen to herself. She did what mommy wanted. She just assumed that she must want what mommy wanted for her. But she discovered this wasn't true. Dahlia wanted something very different.

Dahlia has a mommy wound. She has an overbearing, controlling mother. That is why she feels overwhelmed. She has lived her life to please her mother.

Now Dahlia must confront the False Self she has created. She has to see how she has become passive, withdrawn, submissive. She has to see how she has let mommy run her life.

She has to wake up and say to herself, "I don't want mommy's life. I want my own. I don't want the husband mommy wanted. I want my own husband. I don't want to do what mommy wants anymore. I want to do what I want."

But as soon as she says these words, absolute terror strikes her heart. And that's when she gets in touch with a deeper level of her core belief: This is how she puts it into words:

"If I come into my power, I will lose mommy. Mommy will die or have a nervous breakdown and it will be my fault."

Now that Dahlia wants to take back her life, she is confronting her mommy wound straight on. And it is very intense, because she is experiencing it not just as a forty-two year old woman, but also as a two-year-old child. Because that is when mommy took over her life.

Now we must understand the severity of this, because you would not say at face value that Dahlia was abused. Her mom never hit her or screamed at her. But she also never let Dahlia have her own life.

RECLAIMING OUR POWER

Dahlia gave her power away at age two. Of course, it wasn't her fault. She didn't have much choice. Mommy did not ask for her permission to take over her life. She just did it. And Dahlia let her because she wanted mommy's love. And even if she had wanted to protest, what's a two year old to do?

Now, forty years later, Dahlia is ready to take back her power. And to do so she has got to go right back into the terror of the two year old and confront the self-betrayal, not as a kid, but as an adult. She has to say to mommy, "No. You cannot take over my life. It is my life, not yours, so back off."

Dahlia is lucky because her mother is still alive, so the confrontation can happen in real time. And that is why she is trembling, because this forty-two year old woman is still afraid of her mother. And it takes every ounce of her strength for her to knock on the door to her mother's house.

But that is what she is ready to do. She is ready to reclaim her life.

"Mother, I just wanted you to know that I'm leaving Rick, "she says as soon as her mother pours the tea from the teapot and the two sit down at the kitchen table.

"But Dahlia," her mother says, not missing a beat, "Sometimes things are hard in a marriage and you and Rick can work things out. Not only that, but think of the children. Are you going to break up their home and abandon them?"

"Of course not, Mom, " Dahlia replies, her voice shaking just a little. But taking a deep breath, she continues more forcefully, "I have thought about this a lot, Mom, and I know that you won't agree with my decision. I don't really expect to have your agreement or your blessings. I know that I married Rick for all the wrong reasons. He was the man you wanted me to marry. It was wrong from the start. And now I am finally facing that reality. I have to take my life back, Mom. And I need you to back off. I need you to respect my decision, even if you don't understand it or agree with it."

Now those words don't sound like such a huge deal, but they are Dahlia's DECLARATION OF INDEPENDENCE. They slice through the umbilical cord that has been tying her to her mother for over forty years. They are the words of an empowered woman. They are the words of her True Self.

ELLA'S STORY

Ella and Dahlia have somewhat similar stories, but very different lessons. While Dahlia's empowerment meant that she had to leave her husband whom she did not love, Ella's empowerment required that she make peace with the husband whom she had abandoned six times during the last 13 years of their 23-year marriage.

When Ella wanted to join the Mastery program, I shook my head and said, "I don't know if this program is for you, Ella. If you want to be in this program, you will have to stop running away and begin to face some of your core issues. There are deep wounds here that require healing."

"I am willing to do that," Ella told me. "I am tired of this pain. I am tired of leaving my husband and children. I want to heal my wounds and my relationship with my family."

"Okay, " I told her. So I met with Ella and her husband Isaac.

Both expressed the desire to keep their marriage together. I said to Isaac, "I imagine it has been very painful for you to have your wife leave you and the children so many times, but you must know that there is a reason why she leaves. She doesn't feel safe in the marriage. I can work with Ella to help her break the pattern of running away, but you have to do your part and give her more of a voice in the family. She needs to be seen and heard in the relationship. It can no longer be just on your terms. It must be more equal. Otherwise, this attempt to save the marriage will not work. Are you willing to do your part?"

"Yes," Isaac told me with tears in his eyes. I knew he meant it, but I also knew that it meant reversing some pretty deeply ingrained patterns. It wasn't going to be easy. It wasn't going to happen overnight.

After I accepted Ella into the Mastery Program she began to work diligently on uncovering her Core Wound and the Core Beliefs attached to it. Here is her story.

I came from a family of orphans. My mother's father died when she was 11 years old and her mother became the only provider of the household. My father's father is said to have committed suicide when my father was three years old. His mother died three years later of cancer of the throat.

My father was brought up in an orphanage. As a young adult, he became addicted to having sexual relationships with women. He was not able to be accountable for his actions or to develop his talents, one of which was drawing and making cartoons. He was very meticulous, judgmental and never seemed satisfied. When my mother was seven months pregnant with me she found my father in bed with another woman. She went into early labour and I was born prematurely. After my birth, I stayed in the hospital in an incubator for few weeks and was never breast-fed.

A year later, my parents moved from Canada back to Italy, their country of origin. My father kept on betraying my mother with other women. When I was four years old, my sister was born. She was an extroverted and happy child and I felt that my father preferred her to me, since I was introverted and moody.

When I was six years old my parents divorced. A few years later my father remarried and had two boys. When I was visiting him, I felt like a second-class citizen, as his new wife was very threatened by my sister and me.

My sister was always visiting friends, but I never left the house. I learned to be invisible.

My mother had become the provider of the home just like her mother. I did not have a safe, nurturing, affectionate mother. When I was thirteen my mother had tuberculosis. We were supposed to immigrate back to Canada and I went ahead and lived with my aunt for one year before my mother healed and was allowed into the country.

At the time, I considered my mother my "hero" and my father a stupid, irresponsible fool. In my mind I had cancelled him from my life. Yet my sister adored him and appreciated his sense of humour.

I realized later that I felt abandoned by my father, just as he no doubt had felt abandoned by his parents. Since I was more like my father than like my mother, it is not surprising that I began to act out in ways that were similar to his patterns of avoidance.

I married Isaac because he was safe and would be a good provider. He was a lot like my mother. He liked to be in control and there was not much room for me to grow in the relationship. We had three boys in the first ten years of our marriage. He and the boys were very close and I felt like an outsider. Year by year, I began to feel more and more disconnected from my family. But, instead of speaking up and asking that things change, I ran away.

I see now that this was my father's pattern. I was acting out just as he did. He was abandoned and so he continually betrayed my mother with other women.

During the last thirteen years of my marriage, I have left home six times. But once I made the commitment to the Mastery program, I was determined not to do this again.

My work in the program made it clear that I had a father wound, as well as a mother wound. My father abandoned me and abandoned his own creative talent. I abandoned my children and neglected my talent. Not only did I look like my father, but I also had his gift of drawing and making art.

My father did not encourage me or model for me what it was like to work in a committed way. My mother overprotected me so I never developed any confidence in myself or in my abilities. I was brought up like a trust fund baby without the trust fund so I did not learn how to persevere or manifest my passion.

As I have done my inner child work, I have identified some of my core beliefs that require healing. Here are a few of them:

- I am not good enough.
- I do not fit in.
- I am second class.
- I am stupid, slow.
- I can't do anything on my own.
- I am afraid to be alone.

Recently, as I moved into Level Two of the Mastery program, I uncovered another core belief. This one is a big one:

- *If I come into my power, I will not be loved.*

I now am beginning to realize why I have so much fear about succeeding. To receive my mother's love, I had to be cautious, careful, and obedient. I had to follow the rules and not disappoint anyone. So it was better not to take risks. It was better not to feel my passion or be moved by it.

To this day, when anyone asks me to do anything, I put a huge amount of pressure on myself. I go up into my head and over plan everything. I have become a perfectionist. That's because I feel so insecure. I have no confidence in myself.

And then when I try to perform, I am so fearful and tight, I cannot possibly succeed. I make a mess of things. And I am merciless with myself. Instead of learning from my mistakes and trying again, I run away and try to be invisible. That is my pattern.

That was my father's pattern too. We abandon others. We abandon ourselves. We run away. We are afraid that if we stay, we will be crucified. People will see our flaws and inadequacies.

I spent thirteen years running all over the globe trying to find happiness outside of myself. It didn't work. I took myself—my consciousness—wherever I went. In the end, I had to come home and face my own fears.

I had to do the work my parents had never done. I had to heal my wounds so that I could learn to show up for myself and for my family.

Gradually, I began to see my patterns of avoidance. I began to look at the False Self that I had created in an attempt to cope with my life.

I realized that I had developed a strong tendency to go up into my head and to avoid my emotions. Those emotions were scary and they made waves and I was always trying to be the "good little girl" who did not make waves.

Because I continued to stuff my emotions, they would rise up suddenly and unpredictably and undermine my life. That's probably why I kept running away. I did not know how to stay and process what I was feeling.

But the Mastery work helped me to learn to stay in my heart and feel my feelings. I learned to begin to hold my fear gently and to listen to the anger and sadness of the wounded little girl within me who was afraid to be herself for fear of being rejected.

The work also helped me learn to slow down. My pattern was to shoot for the stars and, as a result, I would keep failing. I would try to get on the rocket ship to heaven and go fast but then it would crash and I would feel even more wounded. Every time I failed my feelings of unworthiness were reinforced.

Without patience and perseverance, constantly jumping from one project to another, how could I succeed?

I had to learn to crawl and then to walk, and now I am taking small steps, practicing patience, and staying focused on goals. I used to go crazy biting my own tail! Now, I am experiencing many small victories. And my confidence in myself is building.

In the past, when my marriage was in crisis, I would go into a total panic. I wanted to leave but I felt powerless to support myself. I needed Isaac to take care of me. He was like my mother. He and she were the rock. Without the rock, I would be overwhelmed by the waves of life.

As I have learned to take the small steps and to build my confidence, I can more easily imagine taking care of myself. I have learned to take risks without putting a huge amount of pressure on myself, and I have had several small successes going out into the world and sharing my gifts.

I have also returned to making art again and this is giving me great joy. I am seeing how I can use art to empower people like myself who have difficulty accessing their emotions. I love coming up with visual exercises and tools that help people access and begin to heal the wounded child within.

I can see that my father wound is healing. I am learning to show up for myself and others. I am beginning to trust my gifts. And I am gaining confidence in myself. I am even able to stand up for myself when I feel that others are crossing my boundaries. That would have been unthinkable just a year or two ago.

In addition, I am healing my mother wound. I am learning to be gentle and nurturing with myself and with others. I know how to hold my little girl and listen to her. We are very connected now. She tells me exactly what she feels, because she knows that I will listen to her.

My relationship with my children has also improved greatly. They were understandably distrustful and angry with me for the times when I left them. But I have rebuilt the trust. They now know that I am not going to leave. They are able to turn to me for support and nurturing. I have at last become the Mother.

All my life I have felt more masculine than feminine. I have dressed like a man, hiding my womanly shape. But now all that is changing. As I connect with the Mother, my feminine nature is coming forth. For the first time in my life, I am able to wear a dress.

Isaac sees this and loves it. Our sex life is much more fulfilling. And he is beginning to relax and trust. He knows that I am not going to leave him. I see the little kid in him opening up. He doesn't need to be so controlling of me or of the children.

Our relationship is not perfect. We still have challenges. But today he tells me now much he appreciates me and values the gifts that I bring to the family. I no longer feel like a stranger in my own house. I feel that I am in my right place.

I am also stepping into my role as a leader in the Mastery community. As I continue to heal and to surrender to the power of love, I am beginning to embody this beautiful Mother energy.

Just last week I went to see my aunt who is 82 for her birthday and I started to caress her back with both my hands. I was just being loving with her. Then, shortly after I touched her, she said, "What is this energy you have in your hands? It is so warm, and gentle. Please come more often to do this to me."

In so many ways now, my life is being transformed. I am not the only one who feels this. My friends and family also feel it. And the mirror they are holding up to me is a gentler one than the one I used to see myself in before my core wounds began to heal.

OUR STORY OF SELF-BETRAYAL

The stories of Dahlia and Ella make it clear that we can heal our core wounds and take our power back. We can stop living the lives that others want us to live. We can stop betraying ourselves or running away from the people we love.

Everyone's story of self–betrayal is a little bit different, but we can map the overall territory. Here are some of the landmarks we can see.

1. ***We Deny our Pain.***
    We pretend that we are not in pain, or we medicate our pain with drugs or alcohol, or cover it up through workaholism, sex addiction or some other compulsive behavior.

2. *We Hide our Shame/Unworthiness.*

We judge ourselves harshly, but we suffer in secret. We don't let others know how badly we feel. We feel like we don't fit, that we are not like others. They seem to be happy and well adjusted, while we feel that there's something wrong with us, like a screw that's loose or in the wrong place. It keeps rattling around inside, but we don't know how to find it or put it back where it belongs.

3. *We Wear a Mask/Create a Persona.*

We find ways to appear normal and to trick others into believing that all is well with us. We know how to make the surface of our lives look good. We may even begin to believe our own lies and deceptions.

4. *We Shame and Blame others and Refuse to Take Responsibility for our Triggers.*

Instead of feeling our shame/guilt, we project it onto others. We blame other people, instead of taking responsibility for our own thoughts, feelings, and actions.

5. *We Betray Ourselves/Others.*

We create a False Self and live within its prison walls. We become a victim and give away our power. Or we become a victimizer and try to take away the power of others.

OUR STORY OF HEALING AND EMPOWERMENT

On the other hand, the story of healing and empowerment can be mapped as well. Here are some of its key components.

1. *We Acknowledge our Pain.*

   We acknowledge our fear and our pain first to ourselves and then to others. We find the root of our suffering. We identify our Core Wound, our Core Beliefs, and our Reactive Behavior Patterns.

2. *We Uncover our Shame/Unworthiness.*

   We make friends with the Wounded Child Within. We learn to love and accept all of ourselves, including the parts that scare us and make us feel uncomfortable.

3. *We Take off our Mask and Get Real.*

   We have the courage to be honest and authentic with ourselves and others. We accept our humanness and our imperfection. We see how we have betrayed ourselves and begin to take back our power.

4. *We Take Responsibility.*

   We pay attention to our emotional triggers and take responsibility for what we are thinking, feeling, or doing. This enables us to stop shaming and blaming. It frees us to create more mutually satisfying relationships with others where boundaries are honored and respected.

5. *We See and Treat People as Equals.*
    We no longer give our power away or attempt to control others. We step into our power and purpose and encourage others to do the same.

Let's see how Dahlia and Ella show up on the journey from self-betrayal to healing and empowerment.

1. *Moving from Denying Pain to Acknowledging it*
    Both Dahlia and Ella were in dysfunctional relationships. They finally acknowledged their pain and decided to do something about it. Dahlia did not want to live a dishonest life married to a man that she did not love. Ella wanted to stop leaving her husband and children every time she got scared.

2. *Moving from Denying Shame to Uncovering it*
    Both Dahlia and Ella felt terrible about themselves, but they suffered silently. It wasn't until they came into the Mastery Program that they realized that other people were in the same boat. The program provided a safe place to look at their wounds and bring love to them.

3. *Moving from Wearing a Mask to Taking it off*
    Dhalia had the perfect family and everyone saw her as the perfect wife and mother. But underneath the surface, she felt miserable. Wanting to please her parents she kept the mask in place until it was unbearable to her. It took great courage for her to let everyone know that she wanted a divorce.

Ella took off her mask when she left her husband the first time. Her life was out of control and she wasn't fooling anyone. She tried to find a new mask as a spiritual seeker traveling around the globe, but it didn't work. The pain came back and she asked for help.

4. *Moving from Denying to Taking Responsibility*
Dahlia felt that she had no choice but to live out her mother's dream until she realized that she was betraying herself. Then she realized that she did have a choice and she would have to exercise it.

Ella realized that she had left a wake of pain behind her as a result of her reactive behavior pattern of running away. Instead of continuing to blame her husband, she decided to take responsibility for changing her behavior and healing her pain.

5. *Moving from Victimhood to Empowerment*
Both Dahlia and Ella decided to take charge of their lives, make their own decisions, and to seek truth, equality and intimacy in their partnerships. Both let go of their victimhood and their patterns of self-betrayal and empowered their True Self to step forward.

PART 4

Three Stages of Healing
& Transformation

Some of us are attached to the attention
the wound gives us. We make it our identity.
This is counterproductive and regressive.

We take the journey into the dark tunnel of the psyche
not to make our home in the wound but to heal it.

The Three Stages

There are three stages in the process of healing and transformation.

The first stage is primarily about personal healing and receiving love from others. The second stage is about personal empowerment and learning to be equals in our relationships with others. And the third stage is about service and facilitating healing for others.

Each of these stages requires a certain type of growth from us. And each stage has clear obstacles that can hold back our progress on the path.

Stage One: Personal Healing

The personal healing process requires us to identify and heal our core wounds and change our core beliefs about ourselves. To do this work, we must stop hiding and become visible and vulnerable. We have to take down our masks and accept our humanness. We need to share our pain, our shame, and our grief with others. In the process, we come out of our isolation and discover spiritual community with others.

The result of Stage One is that we remove our shame and open our hearts to receive love. The more love we let in the more our core wounds heal and the more we change our core beliefs about ourselves and others. Then, we are ready to move out of our patterns of self-betrayal and victimhood.

There are many obstacles that come up in this stage of the healing process. Here are a few of them.

Obstacle: We Deny Our Pain or Have Trouble Accessing it.

Sometimes our pain is fairly deeply locked away. We develop a really strong adult mask with all the accompanying coping skills. We know some of the things that wounded us as children, but we cannot access the emotions around them. We learn to intellectualize and rationalize everything. We can even talk about our pain eloquently, but we cannot feel the abandonment or the betrayal we experienced as kids. We have to sit there a very long time, and listen to many people's stories, before something triggers us at a deep level and we open up.

Very often, if we have a strong mask, we get impatient with the process and begin to make judgments about others who are experiencing the pain of their wound. "Why don't they just get on with it?" we ask. We think that they are just crybabies who don't want to grow up and get over their past. "I'm tired of hearing only about people's pain," we complain. "I want to hear about their joy and their successes also."

We want to be pumped up and motivated so that we can stay on task in our lives. We want to work and be successful. The last thing that we want to do is take time to cry or feel our pain.

As a result, we don't go very deep into the work. We detach from our healing community or leave it before we have reached into the depths of our hearts.

If we are lucky, we will get triggered before we leave. Our denial will be compromised and our mask will shatter. It isn't a pretty sight, but it is an extraordinary blessing. Without this stroke of luck, we might require a heavy charge of dynamite to dislodge our disguise and stop us from going on with business as usual.

Obstacle: We Run Away from Love.

Some of us have no trouble accessing our pain, but the depth of it takes us aback. Even though we may have seen others sobbing when they touch their wound, we never imagine that we will do the same.

If our pain is deep and we have been sitting on it for a while, we can have some pretty strong releases. When that happens, we need lots of support. Often, we feel humiliated or embarrassed about our display of emotion. We feel exposed and alone. We feel that everyone is judging us. That isn't the case, but we will not believe otherwise because we judge ourselves harshly.

Since our pattern is to run when we get scared, we head for the exits. We sneak out of the group, saddle up our horses and gallop away.

If we go home without support, we may fall apart and there may not be anyone there to help us. So our guides and mentors try to intercept us and let us know that what we are feeling is natural. We aren't the only ones who have felt exposed when we have shared something that used be locked away in the privacy of our hearts.

Still, our shame runs very deep. We believe that "If you really knew who I am and what I feel, you would hate me." We don't believe that other people could accept someone who has the demons that we have. Yet if we stay in the circle long enough, we learn that everyone has them in one form or another. We see that we are not alone in our pain or in our self-criticism.

Sometimes when we go from the safety of the circle back home into our lives, we crash. There is a stark difference between the love and acceptance in the community and the judgment and distrust we encounter at home and at work.

We have learned how important it is to create a system of support for us when we go home so that we don't crash and disconnect from the love we so badly want. It is not easy to do this. But we know that it is essential for this work.

In time, we learn to trust the safety of the circle. We know that there is a place we can go where it is safe to be who we are, safe to be with our pain, safe to cry our tears, safe to own our self-hatred. That safe place begins in the circle, but we gradually begin to internalize it. We learn how to hold our own experience compassionately. And then we realize that the circle is not just in our community, but it has come into our heart.

Obstacle: We get stuck in blame.

Sometimes once we have accessed our pain we get stuck in blaming the people who hurt us. We think that by making them wrong it makes us right. We think this is the way that we will restore our innocence. But it doesn't work that way.

Blaming others does not release us from our pain. Indeed, it only intensifies our pain and becomes our justification for holding onto it. In this way, it delays our healing.

We cannot heal until we accept what happened, forgive ourselves for our part in it, and stop blaming our victimizers. Of course, forgiving them is not so much a gift to them as it is a gift to us. When we forgive them, we give ourselves permission to heal and move on.

When we refuse to forgive, we build a whole new mask. It is the mask of "The Victim." This mask tells everyone, "Look at me. I'm special because I was wounded. Pay attention to me."

Building this new "victim" mask is the wounded child's delusional attempt to take charge of his own healing process. Of course, this tactic fails miserably because the wounded child does not know how to heal. Yes, he wants attention/approval, but if he gets addicted to it, his growth will be arrested and the wound will not be healed.

In the beginning of the healing process, it is important that we listen to the wounded child. She has not had a voice in the past and we want to make sure her voice is heard. We encourage the child to share her pain so that it will not be internalized.

But at a certain point, we stop focusing on the wound itself and learn to bring love to it. In order to do that, we have to stop feeling sorry for ourselves and give up being a victim.

Clearly, some people are addicted to the attention the wound gives them. They make the wound their identity. They make a career, if not a life, out of being wounded. Not only that, some of them become teachers and therapists and encourage others to do the same.

All this is counterproductive and regressive. We take the journey into the dark tunnel of the psyche not to make our home in the wound but to heal it.

Obstacle: We Remain a Victim or a Victimizer.

When we refuse to bring love to our wounds we remain victims or victimizers. We beat up on ourselves or we beat up on others.

Most people on the planet are in one category or the other. They either give their power and their responsibility away to others or they take inappropriate power and responsibility away from others.

Victims lack the father energy and cannot stand up for themselves. Victimizers lack the mother energy and cannot nurture themselves. Typically, victims attract victimizers and victimizers attract victims. While this seems to be a deadly set-up, it is actually the crucible in which each learns what s/he has come here to learn. The victim learns to say "No" to abuse, manipulation and control and the victimizer learns to say "Yes" to nurturing, acceptance and love.

All victimizers were once victims. They are simply re-enacting what was done to them.

What is the life lesson for the victim?

It is "Don't be a door mat. Don't give your power away to others. Stand up for yourself. Ask for what you want. Be committed to yourself."

What is the life lesson for the victimizer?

It is "Don't compensate for your powerlessness by trying to control others. Let others be. Stop trying to fix them, save them, or make them love you. Love cannot be won by force, so stop demanding. Learn to respect people's boundaries. Learn to soften and admit your own need for love and affection."

Neither victims nor victimizers understand how to love themselves. They are alike in that each is seeking love through the other. One wants to be saved; the other wants to be the savior. That is why they match.

The beauty and the irony, of course, is that each needs to learn the same thing. Each needs to learn to bring love to him or herself.

Working with Those who Get Stuck.

Recently, in one of our support sessions for mentors, the image of a freight train came up. The freight train is carrying all of our stored pain and self-betrayal. It is letting out a loud whistle, blaming, shaming and complaining. One of our mentors said that after a recent counseling session she felt as if she had been run over by such a train.

We need to remember that it isn't easy to stop a freight train that is going sixty miles per hour. Even after the engineer applies the breaks, it takes a long time for the train to slow down. In the same way, people do not quickly shift out of victim mode. It takes a while for them to stop blaming and to learn to take responsibility for what they are creating in their lives.

The first thing that we have to do when we hear the freight train coming is "get out of the way!" We don't want to be run over and crushed by another person's negativity. We don't want to try to reason with the person and say, "There's no reason to run me over." We just have to get out of the way.

And then we can observe, "I can see how painful this is to you. Is this the way that you want it to be?" If the person says, "No," then we ask, "What can you do to slow the train down so that you can shift it to another track?"

Sooner or later we have to tell people the truth. It is their responsibility to heal. And the first thing they have to do if they want to heal is to stop blaming others and complaining about how terrible their life is. Sooner or later, after they have told their story and cried all their tears, they have to drop the story. Telling it over and over again is not empowering to themselves or to others.

We don't help others when we sit there and listen to them complain. If they are going to grow we have to confront them with the truth. We have to ask, "Whose life is this and who is responsible for it? Whose job is it to stop the broken record from playing? Whose job is it to slow the train down and begin to shift it to a different track?"

We have to help our clients see the way in which they give their power away and hold onto their victimhood. We have to help them see how they create a "no win" situation in their lives. When they say to us, "I'm damned if I do and damned if I don't" we must begin to ask, "Why did you set it up that way?"

We are all responsible for what we are creating in our lives. Seeing things in a "no-win" manner cannot empower us to make any kind of meaningful change in our lives. To bring change, we must believe that change is possible.

A real friend or mentor does not support people in their self-betrayal. S/he tells them, "The way you are thinking concerns me. It seems to me that you are giving your power away. You are blaming others for your pain and not taking responsibility. You are so convinced you are right that this will probably become a self-fulfilling prophecy."

Often our lives become the way that we think they are. That

is because to a certain degree reality seems to conform to our expectations. We expect it to be bad and it is. And then we say, "You see, I told you that is the way it would be!"

If we want things to be different, we need to allow for a different possibility. Instead of saying "If it's not white, it will be black," we can try to discover some of the colors in between. There is a rainbow there that we are not allowing ourselves to see. We are the ones who limit our experience and we need to see that.

We also need to learn to get out of our own way. Life is usually not even half as hard as we make it out to be. Most of our suffering is self- created.

The work of self-transformation asks us to stop complaining and feeling sorry for ourselves. It asks us to stop seeking attention and making a new mask out of our woundedness. It asks us to drop our sad story and stop making excuses for why we can't take charge of our lives.

Each of us has a freight train that is carrying us away from life and running over all who get in its way. The question is "Do we want to stay on that train?"

If we insist on being a victim, the only friends that we will have will be other victims. Is that what we want?

Stage Two: Empowerment

Stage Two of the process of transformation is all about letting go of the False Self and connecting with the True Self. In this Stage, we end our self-betrayal and step into our power as authentic people.

We learn to establish appropriate boundaries with other people so that we are able to make our own decisions and they are able to make theirs. We stop giving our power away or taking power away from others. We take responsibility for all of our experiences, good and bad, and we expect others to do the same.

We no longer project our shame onto others, but continue to heal our wounds by practicing forgiveness of ourselves and others on a regular basis. When we are triggered by others, we own the triggers and see what parts of ourselves remain unhealed and in need of love and acceptance.

We take the small steps necessary to develop our gifts and to share them with others. We no longer shoot for the stars, but set realistic goals that we can achieve. We take reasonable risks, learn from our mistakes and hone our skills so that we can be successful in the world.

The stage is all about Self-Empowerment. It helps us embrace our gift and learn to give it. It strengthens us and prepares us to serve.

Obstacle: We feel Special/Make Others Special.

One of the obstacles that we encounter in Stage Two is that we compare ourselves to others and believe that our gift is not as good as, or that it is better than that of others. Either undervaluing or overvaluing our gift makes it difficult for us to give it successfully. In the former case, we don't trust the gift or have the confidence to offer it. In the latter case, we force the gift on others even when they are not interested in receiving it.

Developing a healthy relationship to our gift requires that we accept it gratefully and give it in a natural and spontaneous way. We don't minimize or exaggerate our talents and abilities. We realize that everyone is special or no one is special. But nobody is more special than anyone else.

When we believe our gift to be better than or less than that of others, we can be sure that our ego is managing our gift and this is doomed from the start. The ego supports only the False Self. It cannot serve the True Self and so it cannot give the gift. Only the True Self can give the gift.

Obstacle: We Try to Skip Steps.

One of the things that happens when the ego tries to take charge of our gift is that it tries to make us go faster than we know how to go. It puts a lot of pressure on us to succeed as quickly as possible. We are always in a hurry to reach the goal and, as a result, we make lots of mistakes.

We don't take the time to practice. We forget that being good at anything requires patience and persistence. Without learning these skills, we cannot reach our goal.

The ego is always buying a ticket on the rocketship to heaven (see Raimonda's image on the following page). It is not content putting one foot in front of the other. As a result, it often makes a great show at the beginning, blasting off with fire and fanfare. But it generally comes down to earth as fast as it leaves the ground. And the results are often catastrophic.

Most of us simply cannot skip steps. We must learn to chop wood and carry water. We have to learn to walk before we run. We have to practice and acquire skill and dexterity. Then, when we are skillful and confident, we can take the world by storm, but not until.

The Rocketship to Heaven (Collage by Raimonda Pironti)

If we try to do it before we have the skill or the confidence required, watch out! Failure is the inevitable price of bravado, carelessness and lack of preparation. When we have inflated expectations, we generally get our bubble burst.

For some of us, it is not a question of going forth to make a big splash before we are ready, but of not going out at all. Fear holds us back. The obstacles to the journey seem much larger than they are. So we procrastinate. We cannot even take the first step.

We also need to learn to take little steps toward the goal. When we take little steps, we don't have to feel overwhelmed or intimidated by the task at hand. We don't have to put unnecessary pressure on ourselves.

Obstacle: We Cling to Security/Remain Co-dependent.

Another obstacle to our empowerment is that we try to hang onto the crutches we have walked with in the past. We continue to let other people do it for us, instead of taking the risk ourselves. That, of course, begs the point.

We cannot be independent and co-dependent at the same time. We can't make our own choices if we are always consulting our parents or other authority figures in our lives.

If the wound has really healed, we won't need those crutches any more. We can throw them away and begin to walk. It may be a little difficult at first, but it will get easier with each step.

It takes courage and determination to become self-reliant when we are used to depending on others. But we need to push through the initial terror. We need to know that our lives will not fall apart even if we make a mistake or a wrong move.

Babies would never learn to walk if they couldn't deal with falling down at first. And it is no different for adults. We need to learn to do it by ourselves, even if it is difficult, even if we fail initially.

If we persevere, we will see that we can survive the inevitable falls and mishaps. We can become more skillful and resilient with each fall and our confidence can grow.

We cannot hold onto the False Self and claim the True Self at the same time. We have to let one go and embrace the other. If we hold onto the limitations of the past, we will recreate the past. If we let the past go, we can step into a new and different future.

A prison is a very secure place, but we don't want to spend our lives there. So we have to take a risk. We have to scale the walls of the prison and break free.

The empowered person we are becoming is completely different from the person who lived in sacrifice and self-betrayal. Indeed, these people live in different worlds.

In the past, we felt that we had no choice. Now we know that we do. So we have to decide what we want. Do we want the freedom to choose and the responsibility for our choices or do we want to let others make the choice and take the praise or the blame?

Those who hang onto their security or let others decide for them stay safe within the prison walls. Society feeds them and houses them, but they have only the shadow of a life.

They do not live joyfully or passionately. How could they? Their lives do not belong to them.

Stage Three: Service
& Facilitating Healing for Others

The third stage of the journey of transformation involves stepping into the fullness of our power and life purpose, actively sharing our gifts with others, and helping others to heal. This is the stage of the journey where we give back to others the love and support we have received.

Serving others creates a renewal of the spiritual energy in our lives. By giving confidently and without conditions, we receive a kind of love and support back from the universe that is qualitatively different from anything we have yet experienced. It is as if the Divine is directly communing with us, heart to heart, and we can feel its power and protection.

The more we are able to surrender, the more we are able to become an instrument, a hollow reed that the Divine can play. We are the flute that echoes in the canyon. We are not the one who plays it.

"Not my will but Thy Will be done" becomes our modus operandi. We are no longer trying to run our lives at the ego level. We are letting Spirit within guide us.

As we deepen in our capacity to surrender, great works are done through us. We are amazed at what happens when we just show up and do the best that we can. Our surrender creates an abundant harvest all around us.

The power of love reaches out in waves to all who are reaching for it. Prayers are answered. Miracles are witnessed. Love is spontaneously given and received.

This continues until our ego rises up and wants credit, ownership or control over what is happening. Then the miracles stop. The energy of giving and receiving gets blocked.

It continues as long as we stay in our hearts and in the moment. As soon as we go up into our heads and try to figure everything out, as soon as we start worrying about the past or future, grace seems to evaporate and, all of a sudden, everything gets hard.

Obstacle: We try to control; We get in the way.

We forget that God is making the sound through us. We think that we are the one blowing the flute and then the sound stops. That is Spirit's way of reminding us that none of this can happen without our surrender.

Let us not be surprised if our ego comes up and we want to take control. Let us not be surprised if we become selfish and want personal recognition. These things will happen. None of us are completely healed. Even though we have moved forward to serve, there are still remnants of our unworthiness lurking within. These remnants will continue to surface so that we can heal them.

Just because we are serving does not mean that our healing process is complete. Indeed, in some respects, our healing process intensifies. In endeavoring to give to others, all our remaining insecurity comes up. We can no longer hide it or stuff it.

We know that every obstacle to love must be removed so that the channel can be cleared. The reed must become hollow again so that the music can resume.

Once we have experienced God's fiery love and abundance, nothing less will do. We are not satisfied with conditional love. We know that we must dissolve all these blocks to the power and presence of love. We must become empty so that the Spirit of God can express through us.

Service gives us the opportunity to go even deeper into the heart of love. But it also requires something from us. We have to let go at a deeper level. We have to surrender and trust the Divine to work with and through us. We have to keep getting out of the way.

Obstacle: We become attached to our gifts.

Still another obstacle—not unlike the one above—is that we become attached to the way that we give our gifts and/or to the way they are received by others. This happens because we mistakenly think that the gifts belong to us. That is not an accurate understanding.

The gift is entrusted to us for safe keeping, for nurturing and development and ultimately for expression. But it is not our gift per se. We are the giver of the gift, not the creator of it. The gift comes from Spirit. It merely comes through us.

We do not know how or when the opportunity to give the gift will come. Our job is simply to be ready when it does come. And we do not know how the gift will be given or received. Our job is to trust that it is happening appropriately, even when it is not meeting our expectations.

All our expectations simply get in the way of the process of giving and receiving. When we want to give in a certain way, it is hard to give. When we want to receive in a certain way, it is hard to receive.

Both giving and receiving require openness and trust in the process as it unfolds. They require that we see our expectations and release them. We will not be able to control the process, no matter how much we want to. The process defies control. It requires surrender.

Our job is not to become God, but to serve God. And to serve God we must get out of the way.

God, on the other hand, has already gotten out of the way. He gave us free will. He refused to control us. He gave us a choice.

We must do the same thing with the gifts that have been entrusted to us. We must let them go and do what they are designed to do.

All gifts carry an energy and an intention. Let us trust this and let the gift do its work. It is impossible to give the gift and hold onto it at the same time. To give it, we must let it go.

We will never know, nor can we anticipate, what the gift will do. We may have given a talk to a stone-cold audience, only to find out many years later that this talk saved someone's life.

We cannot evaluate the gift. That is not our job. Our job is simply to give the gift freely, without strings attached.

Its value will become clear in time, first to others, and then maybe to us. For all that we give returns to us sooner or later.

Let us lay our expectations down now and trust the process. That is the best attitude we can bring to service.

Jesus told us that we would know the tree by its fruits. But that cannot happen as long as we hold onto those fruits. We must let them fall from the tree when they are ready.

Some will fall to the ground and become fertilizer and seed for next year's harvest. Others will nourish the people who find them and eat them.

We cannot know who will come and be served and who will come and find the branches bare. That is not up to us.

The people we thought would be first in line to take the fruit from the tree will show up last, or not at all. And the ones we expected to go hungry will arrive in time to take the fruit when it is ripest and most juicy.

Life is not linear, nor is it predictable. That is why we must release our expectations. If we don't, we will continually be disappointed.

What comes around goes around, but it often takes a long time. Let's not hold our breath waiting for it.

Breathing in, we accept what comes. Breathing out, we let it go. Acceptance and surrender are the engines of grace in this world. Let us submit to them and save ourselves a lot of struggle.

Obstacle: We try to feed our ego.

Our gift does not feed our ego. If we try to use it to feed our ego, it will not be easily shared with others.

The gift is not given to benefit us, but to benefit others. Of course, if it benefits others, it will eventually benefit us. But don't hold your breath! And don't give to get back because that doesn't work.

The gift must be freely given or it cannot help anyone. A gift that is given with strings attached never reaches the receiver. It becomes a boomerang that returns and smacks the giver in the face.

Our gift will not bring us personal credit or if it does it will come at a price. We would be smart not to be attached to name and fame, even if the gift seems to come with it.

Whatever we become attached to becomes a cross that we must bear. At first it may appear to be a pedestal that we mount to great veneration and applause, but it won't be long before we have to drag that heavy lumber with us up the hill. That's when we realize it is not a pedestal but a cross, and the people who have come to watch are not our fans, but our enemies.

Our gift is given not to lift us up, but to uplift others. If we try to make it be about us, instead of about them, we will turn the gift into a spear that will aggravate our wound of unworthiness.

If that happens, let's try to learn from it. Some of us have to revisit the wound in powerful ways in order to finally heal it.

For most of us, the lesson is a simple one. We need to turn our swords into pruning hooks and get busy trimming the branches of the tree. Hard work insures a healthy harvest.

When we show up humbly and go to work along side others, the gift is effortlessly given. Miracles happen and people are astonished.

Only the wise Taoist master notices that the soil has been lovingly tilled and the branches carefully pruned. He is the only one who is not surprised by the sweetness of the fruit or the fragrance of the blossoms.

When he looks down at his hands, he sees the calluses where the rake was held and the scrapes where the branches bit into the skin. He knows the price of the miracle and he is happy to pay it.

May we know it too! May we admire the harvest and remain humble. May we be content with our labor and unattached to the results.

That way we cannot be disappointed. That way there are no disasters or defeats, but only victories!

PART 5

Real Life Stories

I came face to face with the hurt little girl who felt she was bad and could do nothing right. I took her up in my arms and held her with compassion.

I asked for her forgiveness. I cried an ocean of tears. Gradually, my shell of denial began to crack open.

The Healing Power of the Wound

The wounds that we give and receive either destroy us or they wake us up. If we allow ourselves to feel the pain of the wound, deeply and profoundly, our only choice is to wake up.

If we stuff the pain or medicate it, the pain becomes chronic. In that case, the wound is hidden and goes unhealed.

When we look at all the brutality that exists in the world, it seems that the life is playing a rather cruel joke on us. The pain seems both endless and mindless. It goes on and on, passed from one generation to another.

However, it only takes one member of a family to stand up and say "I cannot stand this pain anymore. I must find the cause of it and heal it once and for all." That family member can end the pain not just for herself, but also for her children and her children's children.

The choice to feel our pain and heal our wounds is a choice each one of us will make or refuse to make. If we choose to make it, the candle of hope will be lit for countless others. If we choose not to make it, the world becomes a little darker and more dreary.

Lest all this seem too abstract, let me share with you two real life stories from our healing community.

MARYANN'S STORY

MaryAnn came into our Spiritual Mastery Community about two years ago. It didn't take long to identify MaryAnn's core wound, because she was carrying it like a huge boulder on her shoulders. As heavy and as uncomfortable as was for her to carry that stone, putting it down was no easy task.

MaryAnn wore a very good mask. She was a successful businesswoman and had an engaging personality. She was able to make people feel at ease and they loved to be in her presence. She was able to take care of herself and to be generous with her friends. Not many people knew that, beneath the mask, she was in dire pain and distress.

MaryAnn had been reading my books for years and she heard my call to my readers to come to a retreat and begin the process of deep emotional healing and transformation. Her initial retreat experience helped her to experience the profound power of unconditional love and acceptance. Yet it also made her intensely aware of the block to love that stood like an impenetrable steel wall in the middle of her heart.

One day MaryAnn came to me to request in-depth counseling. Up until this time, she had never disclosed her wound. "You have to promise me that when you hear my secret, you will not judge me or reject me," she told me.

"Okay," I told her. "I can do that."

MaryAnn's request for therapy was a brave one. It said to me, "I cannot live with this wall any more. I am ready to take it down. I am ready to clear this space so that love can enter." And so began a two-year process of healing that, at times, was quite harrowing. Indeed, there were many times when I wondered if MaryAnn would make it all the way through the dark tunnel into the light.

MaryAnn tells the story best:

My deep root of shame and unworthiness started as a small child. I lived in the country and I had a dog and cats and some other critters to play with, but I did long for girlfriends instead of dolls for playmates.

The marriages of my two older sisters left me feeling vulnerable to a mother who was loving and gentle one moment and raging and threatening the next. By age six, I was ready to get to school and so excited I could not stand it. I remember the special clothes and great anticipation because I was going to make FRIENDS.

However, my first week of school was to become a slow descent into hell. After a two-mile bike ride, I arrived at school wearing my pretty, new clothes. I was in a classroom with five grades. My name was printed on the top right corner of my desk. One day at the end of the first week, my young teacher was giving a music lesson and I noticed the girl ahead of me drawing circles around her name. It looked very nice, so I doodled circles around mine too.

Well "Miss Crazy" saw me and over she came. She told me to stand up in front of the class and slapped my hand. I was shamed and embarrassed in front of all the new friends that I so wanted to make.

My teacher was as hard on me as my mother. It seems I went from one unbalanced woman to another. Anyway, I didn't think I wanted to go back to school. I was ready to be a six year old "dropout."

Towards the end of the month I finally made a friend, the daughter of the country doctor, and she lived in a house about half way to mine. One day on the way home she invited me to stop and play at her house. I said, "Oh yes" and when her mother asked if my mother knew where I was I said, "Yes she does." Well, of course, my mother had no idea where I was, but somehow she found me, pulled me out of that house, and gave me a really good thrashing in front of my new friend. I was so humiliated that I wished that I was dead.

As a teenager I felt stupid, ugly, full of self-loathing and unworthiness. When I was seventeen and living off and on at home, my mother and I had a terrific fight. For some reason she thought I was a tramp and I was hurt and angry. I had no boyfriend, but I did have a mad crush on a married guitar player, so I called him and purposefully went out and slept with him. Soon afterward, I became pregnant.

So I went to a neighboring convent and, four months later, I had a very sweet baby boy. Two lovely student nurses would sneak him in so that I could hold him, but when they told me they couldn't do it anymore I checked out of there in a hurry. I was told to pretend it didn't happen. There was to be no regrets, no grieving, no baby! I was to put my high heels on and go back to work.

Life was no better living back with Mom and Dad. I had to figure how to get out and stay out. I saw that my older sisters were left pretty much alone to live their lives once they got married and so that was my direction. Now all I needed was a husband and he turned out to be the baby's father's best friend. I did not know him well but I felt confident that I could help him get off probation if he could get me out of the house and away from what I believed to be insane parenting. I married only weeks after knowing this young man, but I would stay out of the marriage bed until I would get comfortable. One year later—New Years Eve – my daughter was born into a family of two emotionally unbalanced young adults.

My mother was so angry that she did not want anything to do

with me and she and my father hated my husband because he was lazy and a drifter. So I had no money, job or support and my handsome husband did not appear to be able to take care of his family. My older sister Ellen invited me to spend a few days with her. I loved her dearly so I went out to her home and watched how wonderful and motherly she was with my baby. I remember wondering how come I didn't look or feel like a mother. It was natural to be married and have a baby, but why didn't it feel right to me?

As my husband could not be trusted or depended upon, I was the one working and leaving my baby with my mother. My husband had a violent temper and if he was around we would get into physical fights. This was not good for either one of us. According to my mother I couldn't do anything right, so one night I said "enough" and I felt the greatest thing I could do for this child who deserved so much better was to turn her over to my very willing sister. I guess one might say I abandoned her but I knew that Ellen would love her dearly and she did for nine months.

Then 35 year old Ellen was rushed to the hospital while three heart specialists and her husband stood helplessly and watched her die. This tragic loss of my dear sister also resulted in the loss of the loving, dependable care of my baby. So I tried to take on motherhood again. I knew it would be tough, but I did not think there was any other solution. Well apparently there was, but it was a solution that would give me the greatest pain and guilt for the rest of my life!

Three weeks later my beautiful 18-month-old baby girl was to drown under a walking bridge that broke while my younger sister was pushing her in a buggy on the way to the park!

I was devastated. I was convinced more than ever before that my mother was right. I WAS A TOTAL FAILURE. My father seemed to be of the same opinion. Indeed, he told me just before *the funeral that I had no right to grieve. For years, I believed him, at least until I began reading Paul Ferrini's work.*

Not many human beings know the depth of my pain or self-condemnation. I have lived for many years on a hidden-away cross, punishing myself in secret. Yes, on the surface, I learned to survive. You might even say that I have been very successful. I have had a great career as a real estate agent. I am loved and appreciated by many friends and colleagues. But, inside of me, a gaping wound was festering and crying out for healing.

It was that wound that I invited Paul Ferrini to witness with me. "Promise me," I told him before committing to counseling, "that you will not judge me. I could not bear that!" He promised and, for the next six months, he held a gentle space for me while I began to look at my reactive behaviors and see how they kept me on the cross.

In the process, I came face to face with the hurt little girl who felt she was bad and could do nothing right. I took her up in my arms and held her with compassion. I asked for her forgiveness. I cried an ocean of tears.

Gradually, my shell of denial began to crack open. Paul kept holding the space. He challenged me to tell my story at retreats and to open myself to greater healing. That was terrifying to me. I was so afraid of being judged and rejected by others. But I kept walking through all the doors.

Once during a church service at a retreat in Florida, one of my fellow mastery students took me into her arms and held me as a mother holds her child. I began to sob. I could not stop. Years of stored away pain and self-judgment began to release. It was not easy, I have to tell you. Every time I allowed myself to become visible and vulnerable to my friends and spiritual family, I wanted to run away. Sometimes I would disappear for weeks. Sometimes, I'd be gone for months. But Paul's arms and the arms of my community continued to reach out to me. No matter how scared I got, no matter how triggered, no matter how much pain and unworthiness surfaced, I always found my way back.

Welcome back, MaryAnn," they would tell me. "We love you and we so missed you." And again, the tears would come, but this time they were tears of joy, because I knew that for the first time in my life I had been accepted for the person I am, wounds and all. For the first time in my life, love was offered to me without conditions, and I could not push it away.

I have learned my lessons, you might say, "the hard way." That, I guess, is one of the reasons that we are here: to learn from our mistakes.

Paul likes to call me THE MOTHER. It is hard for me to hear that, because I have felt like such a failure as a mother. But I know why he calls me that.

To heal, I have had to become a Mommy to myself. I have had to learn to wrap my arms around myself and hold myself gently. Today, because I am learning to stop beating myself up, I can show up for all of the wounded and abandoned children out there, because I was one of them. In my own way, I know their pain. And I also know the pain of the parent who abandons a child, because I am one of them. This, I suppose, is what Paul means when he says that the wound and the gift run hand in hand. Where I have hurt most is where I must heal, and that too is where I can best serve others.

THE WOUND AND THE GIFT

I call MaryAnn The Mother because that is her calling and her
life purpose. She has come to earth to learn to be the Mommy.
To do this, she had to set up some hard lessons.

First she had to come into this life through an ambivalent
mommy who was sometimes loving, but frequently cruel to her.

This established MaryAnn's core wound of abandonment.
Whenever she needed her mommy's love, her mommy criti-
cized her and rejected her. Her daddy didn't do much better.

The first traumatic event in her journey to motherhood
happened when she got pregnant and had to give up her baby
boy. In her attempt to escape from her mommy, MaryAnn had
became a mommy who would abandon her baby.

Then she gave birth to her daughter and realized that she
could not take care of her. So she asked for her sister's help rais-
ing the child. Then her sister died. Talk about abandonment!

Again, she tried to be a mommy, and her baby died in an
accidental drowning. The pain of this event was to stay with
MaryAnn all her life. All of her deep-seated shame and unworthiness was wrapped up in this traumatic event.

MaryAnn's core wound was abandonment/criticism/rejection.
Her reactive behavior pattern was to run away and hide. She tried
to run away from her mother. And she tried to run away from
being a mother. MaryAnn carried a huge MOMMY WOUND.

Attached to that wound, was a mountain of shame and guilt.
For MaryAnn was not just dealing with the guilt of running
away. She actually believed that she was responsible for her
daughter's death. In her eyes, she was not only a coward, but
a murderer.

Talk about shame! MaryAnn didn't believe that she had the right to be alive. In her eyes, she was *bad, horrible, unredeemable.*

No wonder she did not want to trust me with her secret. If I had judged her, I would have been pounding the final nail into her suffering body, the nail that would keep her on the cross forever.

That's why I said to her, "MaryAnn, no matter what, I will not judge you. I am putting the nails and the hammer away. You are safe to tell me about your pain. And one of these days you will give yourself permission to come down off the cross."

As she said, it was not easy. At every stage in the healing process, she tried to run away from us. Sometimes, we had to stand in front of her car and plead with her to stay. We didn't want her to leave a retreat after she had just had a huge emotional release, because bringing up her pain left her feeling exposed and even humiliated. We wanted to soften that and help to hold her while she integrated the experience.

We just wanted to love her, but MaryAnn did not always permit it. She would head for the exit and sometimes we couldn't head her off at the pass. Old layers of unworthiness were coming up and she was doing what she had always done from a very early age — she was running away.

Even when she ran, we would call her up to check on her. "You can't push our love away," we all told her. But that didn't mean that she didn't try! Once she told me, "Please leave me alone. I am done with this work. Please respect my decision!"

Of course, we were prepared to let her go if she really needed to go. We knew how difficult and painful it was for her to come back only to see another layer of shame come up for healing. But what was the alternative? She had already opened Pandora's box! And once that box is opened it's impossible to put all of the demons back inside.

Once you have made the decision to heal, anything less than that is not satisfactory. You have to come back and finish the job. And that's what MaryAnn did.

We watched as MaryAnn let out gut-wrenching sobs during the church service. At another time, we witnessed her terror as she began to gurgle and choke, reliving her daughter's death by drowning. And we watched when a young woman — who was the age her daughter would have been had she lived — reached out and took MaryAnn in her arms and held her as a Mommy would hold her child.

Here is what one of the witnesses wrote after seeing the event unfold:

MaryAnn looked at Jenny and said, "You remind me so much of my mother . . . such a sweet, loving face. When I look into your eyes, I feel that I am looking into my mother's eyes." Jenny had the sweetest expression on her face and I just "knew" that something extraordinary was going to happen. I watched as Jenny got up from her seat and went over to MaryAnn and hugged her. Then she sat down and reached up and started to stroke MaryAnn's head and her face and MaryAnn laid her head in Jenny's lap and cried and cried. The rest of us sat there in silence.

I can't speak for everyone else who witnessed it . . . but I sat there in awe. It was one of the most beautiful moments I had ever witnessed.

Jenny holding MaryAnn   Photo: Orion Kovach

That opening to love's presence was the crowning event in MaryAnn's journey to healing. Finally, she had been able to accept Mommy's love, as well as the love of her child. The wall in her heart came down at last, and the love just poured in.

She would never be the same. Her pain had been transmuted and her shame was dissolved.

Later, MaryAnn had a dream that she shared with me:

> *I woke up dreaming that I was in a house by the water. There was a younger person there and I remember going to the edge of the water and this person jumped in and I was able to get her out and dry her off. And I told this person "we must go to the bridge to get to the other side."*
>
> *Bridges are important to me because my daughter fell off a bridge and drowned. And here I am leading this other person to the bridge. I now believe LOVE is the bridge.*

The dream confirmed the healing. But there were to be more confirmatory dreams. Here is another one:

> This morning I woke up dreaming that my parents gave birth to a baby and my mother said that she was turning this baby over to me to raise. I am wondering why they would do this when my mother tells me that they have won the lottery and if I will take care of this baby they will give me a brand new house and the financial support I will need.
>
> I remember looking at this baby thinking do I have it in me to love and care for this child? Can I love this child? Next thing I know I am whizzing around the bay looking for new construction to live in and I remember thinking it must be built right if we are to weather all the storms.
>
> After I woke up, I just lay there with this somewhat crazy dream and then I had the realization that I WAS THE BABY.

Yes, MaryAnn was both the baby and the mother. Healing had come to the divided parts of her psyche. MaryAnn was ready to love and embrace herself unconditionally. She was ready to be the Mommy she had come to earth to be. In the great alchemical furnace, the wound had been transformed. It had become the gift!

NURTURING THE GIFT: CAROLINA'S STORY

Even as a child, Carolina loved art. But her mother, always the practical one, never encouraged her talent. Carolina writes:

> *Ever since I could hold a pencil I was drawing. When I went from primary to secondary school the teacher advised my mom to let me go to a more artistic school. But since that was far away and too difficult to travel to I was sent to a local school. So art school was not in my reach. My mom thought it would be wiser for me to go to a business school. And so I did.*

Like many of us, Carolina buried her gift somewhere in her childhood. She did the practical thing that her mom wanted her to do. She became a stockbroker.

I met Carolina on a recent European tour. In my workshop I talked about our wounds and our gifts and the connection between them and Carolina had a big "ahaa" moment. She had just begun drawing again after years of neglecting her artwork, so she was getting back in touch with her gift. And then she realized that her gift of drawing could be connected to her core wound of abandonment—her father had died when she was only six years old—and she would discover her house of healing. She writes:

> *Paul told us that once we have healed this wound we can help others with the same pain. I thought about the time my dad died. I was only six years old. Those were awful times. Nowhere to hide for me. No one who understood me. I escaped in a fantasy world but I paid a high price for this behavior later in my life. If only there was someone who*

understood me then . . . . And suddenly it came together . . .
the paintings and the wound. Would it not be a great way for
a child to communicate in difficult times through drawing?

Later, another person at the workshop told me about a
school that teaches us how to use art as a tool for healing
(a coincidence?) and he gave me the website so that I could
explore this idea. It felt like I finally found a signpost after
wandering in the wild for a lifetime . . . suddenly there was a
sign with the word "home" on it.

The retreat with Paul really inspired me to pick up my pen-
cils again. Strangely, my drawings all of a sudden had become
different; they looked better to me than they had before.

I went back to my old drawing class. My art-teacher had
moved to a building where psychiatrists work. A woman
working there as a psychiatrist was also in my class. She told
me she was giving a symposium on psychiatric treatment,
and a part of the symposium was about healing and drawing.
When I told her I was interested to do this with children, she
invited me to come to the symposium (another coincidence?).

It still startles me how all things can come together to assist
us in fulfilling our purpose. I guess if God wants us somewhere
and we are willing to go, it doesn't take long for us to get
there.

It is true that God wants us to discover our gift and use it to
help others heal. And we will receive lots of support from the
universe when we are ready to stand in our power and share
our gift.

However, empowerment does not come overnight and healing happens in its own time. After she left her second retreat,
Carolina went into a downward spiral. At that retreat Carolina

has gotten in touch with both her Daddy wound and her Mommy wound. Not only did she feel abandoned by her father who died when she was six, but she also felt emotionally abandoned by her mother.

When her father died, Carolina's mother was feeling her own sense of loss and abandonment. But she didn't have the time to explore those feelings. She had to be tough and determined because she had a family to support. As a result, she was not a nurturing parent for Carolina. At the retreat, Carolina got in touch with her mommy wound and was determined to confront her mother with this new information.

We warned Carolina that this was a set up and that often you don't get the love you want from your actual mommy. Sometimes you have to find another mommy who really understands you to give you the love that you so desperately want.

But Carolina didn't listen. She tried to go to her birth mommy to get the love she didn't get as a kid. And guess what? Things hadn't changed. Mommy still couldn't be understanding and nurturing to her. So then Carolina felt like a jerk that she had asked for nurturing. She began to really beat herself up and all her unworthiness came up.

Friends and community members reached out to her, but Carolina pushed them away. She was a scared little horsie running at break-neck speed in the opposite direction. Yes, she still remembered all the love that she received at the retreat, but her bubble had been smashed at home.

"It's better not to expect anything, than to expect love and be disappointed," she told herself. "I am a loner anyway. I don't need love.

Carolina had given up hope that love was possible for her. I knew I had to reach out to her, so I wrote encouraging her to come to the next retreat. She replied as follows:

Dear Paul,

I cannot do it... I am sorry... All my life I survived by running away. I have this great pain inside me. I think I control it, but it controls me... It is so strong, it is part of me and I have become used to it.... At times it goes away and I am okay, but it comes back to me every time I think I can escape from it... It puts me back in place... and I feel the pain even more than before, like a punishment for my escape.... Like when I came back from Vermont, I paid for being happy there. Do you believe it when I say I wished I never went there because coming back was so hard?

This pain owns me. It takes over... and all the love is gone. I feel no connection with anything. It tells me that I am better off by myself. It tells me "Run, Carolina, run"... and so I do. I run far away from love. Because that is what I fear most. Love... it frightens me. In my mind, it is not real, so I think I am best alone. No one gets hurt that way.

And I just want to die. Death seems like a savior. I hate the world I am in. It is such a bad play to be in. So many people just survive... playing a role. Just like me... running.

I know you know this pain. I see it in your eyes, just as I do in Jesus' eyes... You know it is out there. It takes over people as it has taken over me long ago. All these beautiful spirits lost in pain.

I thank you for caring but please forgive me that I cannot fight it. It is so big, Paul, so very big. I am so sorry.

Carolina

Yes, I knew the pain that Carolina mentioned in the letter. It is the pain and the despair of the human heart when it feels cut off from love and purpose. Carolina is not the only one who has felt this way, although in her darkest moments she might believe that she is the only one who feels that scared and cut off.

In our community, we place a very high value on honesty and authenticity. No one, including Carolina, can come to a retreat and not see the fear, the pain and the shame that all who embark on the healing journey must weather. The storm will come and we want it to, because we do not want to keep these destructive emotions locked in. We want to release them, so that our walls can come down and we can make room for love to enter.

Carolina's email to me was dark and dreary, but I knew another side of her. I knew the little girl that liked to have fun and had a great sense of humor. I decided to try to connect with that side of her. I replied to her email in a tongue-in-cheek manner, encouraging her to hang in there and come to the next retreat.

> Dear Carolina:
> I want you to know that God came to me this morning and told me to make this retreat just for you. We are calling it: *Spiritual Schizophrenia: The Art of Coming Home by Running Away from Yourself.*
> This retreat is mandatory for all scared horsies who are afraid to be loved and run away when you get too close to them. I love this idea, because I truly believe there is a scared horsie in all of us. What do you think? Does it make you want to run away in the opposite direction?

If so, that's great, because the world is round, and after you go through Russia and Hawaii you will eventually get to Florida and can join us there for our retreat.

What say you? Are your bags packed for Russia?

Paul

PS Please rest assured that we will go forward with this enlightening topic, whether or not you come. So—no pressure—no guilt trips—come if you want to—don't come if you don't want to—come if you don't want to—or don't come if you want to. Let's keep all the options on the table!

Giving Carolina permission not to come and trying to bring a little bit of humor to the "scaredy horsie syndrome" seemed to work because after receiving this letter Carolina decided to show up at the next retreat.

Like MaryAnn, Carolina was learning to walk through her pain and her fear. In fact, the two scared horsies connected in a big way at the next retreat. MaryAnn and Carolina left that retreat, arm in arm, heart in heart. MaryAnn signed up to be Carolina's mentor and a new mother-daughter relationship of healing was born.

I have always said that it takes one scared horsie to know another. How can you help another person heal if you have never experienced the kind of wound they have?

There is certain chemistry in the healing process and in our community we are fortunate enough to have the right ingredients. Indeed, the necessary ingredients are out there in many communities. We just need to understand how to put them together.

CONNECTING THE WOUND AND THE GIFT

Carolina is quite blessed to know what her gift is and to be committed to developing that gift and sharing it as a tool for healing. There is no doubt in my mind that she will be working with children using art as a language to help them communicate their deepest emotions. One day, she will help a little girl who has lost a daddy or a mommy, just as she did.

Recently, she shared with me a wonderful painting that she had done for a family of girls who had just lost their favorite horse. This horse had brought much love to the girls and they wanted a painting that would help them remember him.

When I first saw the painting, I immediately recognized all the healing that had happened for Carolina while painting it. She and I both agreed that this was not the scared horsie who runs away, but the empowered horse that stands his ground.

In order to understand what the empowered horse means, you have to understand that he starts as a scared horsie. Here is how Carolina described him in an earlier email:

When I got home I felt really lonely and bad. I felt a great longing to use drugs again to anesthetize the pain and the lonely feeling. I was more down than I was in years.

I realized that I am like a scared horse. Horses are born to run away when danger appears.

Yesterday I was with somebody who told me that my core issue was that I could not love myself. And I know this. That's why I cannot feel real love for anyone, and why I run away from any kind of connection. Running away keeps me safe. Love means hurt for me.

Carolina did not realize how much healing was happening just through her emerging awareness of her reactive behavior pattern and the core wound attached to it. Just being able to name the wound and the reactive pattern was creating the psychological climate in which healing could take place.

Now look at the ceremonial horse that Carolina painted for the girls (see page 112). This is the empowered horse that does not run away. He has learned to stand his ground, to ask for love, and to receive it. There he stands in all of his beauty and integrity, a powerful representation of the True Self.

Here's Carolina's story of how she made the painting:

From the moment I received the picture of the horse from the woman who wanted me to paint him for her girls, this horse showed me his healing gift. The girls received so much love and healing through him and I thought how sad it was that they could be with him only for such a short period of time. (Remember, Carolina had been with her father for such a short period of time too.)

I started drawing him in the beginning of December. I was not very happy then. But I started to paint him anyway because I felt sorry for the girls. From the moment I began painting him, this horse had a mind of his own. He looked very lively to me, although that was not how I felt. And I was surprised that I could paint something so vivid despite this low feeling I had.

In previous drawings I always left the paper color as the background (that was safe as the background could easily ruin the painting), but this horse forced me to paint a background around him. He wanted to be in the world, not floating on an empty page.

Accidentally, I made this big dark cloud above his head. I was not too happy about that but I could not wipe it out.

I wanted to throw the whole painting away and start over again, but the horse told me "Don't." He kept looking straight at me and said, "You will have to learn that things, no matter how ugly they seem to you, can turn into treasures one day. You will learn to see the whole picture, not just the part that you like or dislike. Wholeness is what makes the beauty. Don't focus on one part; focus on the whole." So I did not throw the painting away. I gave him the benefit of the doubt.

Eventually, this horse and I got connected. He kept looking straight at me every time I walked past him. One day I wondered what his name was and I asked the woman; it was Focus (isn't that brilliant?). Gradually the painting was finished and the dark cloud over his head did not look that bad to me anymore.

Then I started to feel attached to the painting and I did not want to give it to the girls anymore. It had become a piece of me. But I realized that by sharing the spirit of Focus in my painting he can reach other people too with his message of healing.

I think Focus has some of the Native American wisdom in his soul. He was an Appaloosa horse (white with spots). This is a Native American breed, so I painted feathers in his hair. They represent his freedom.

Yes, Carolina is right. The horse must have his freedom. However, his freedom no longer carries him away from love, but toward it.

When we face our fears, love and freedom are no longer at odds. They are, indeed, inextricably related. For love must be free or it is not unconditional.

Carolina's painting entitled "Focus"

The love of Carolina's birth mother—like that of any birth mother—was imperfect. Her mother was human, with her own fears, stressors and demons. She had suffered the trauma of her husband's death and she was doing the best that she could. Yes, it is true; her heart did shut down to some extent. She went to work and learned to cope. She was not a monster. She was a human being.

To be sure, she wanted to love her daughter without conditions, but she just couldn't do it. Do you know any parent who could do it, including yourself?

All of us are human. All of us contract in fear and grow walls in our hearts when we have been hurt. That's what happened to Carolina's mom. That's what happened to Carolina.

There is a scared little horsie in all of us who pushes love away or runs away from it. We aren't going to change that.

But we need to make friends with that little horsie, just as Carolina did. We need to establish a bond of trust, so that the horsie learns to stand his ground and ask for the love that he wants. The amazing thing is that when he walks through his fear and makes his request in earnest, the love comes pouring through.

The scared little horsie can have what he wants. He just has to move through his fear of rejection. He just has to take down the wall in his heart.

That is the work of healing we are all engaged in. Carolina took that journey with the help of her gift. She transformed the scared horsie into *Focus*, the ceremonial horse, the native American keeper of wisdom.

Painting *Focus* brought joy and fulfillment not just to Carolina, but to the little girls who had lost their childhood companion. It transformed loss into healing and wisdom.

Now when we look at *Focus*, we can hear him telling us to look at the whole, not just at the part. We can hear him challenging us to accept all of the aspects of ourselves so that we can experience our wholeness and that of others.

PART 6

Existential Wounds

Thanks to the wound, life is either a journey
of alienation or a quest for connection.

Often it starts as one and becomes the other.
The moment when it shifts is usually
a spiritual awakening experience.

Life is a Set-Up

Nobody warns us before we come here, but life is a set-up. The very act of being born is traumatic for everyone. And I mean everyone! I'm not talking just about those who are born premature or with birth defects, those who are breech or taken out with forceps. I am not just talking about those whose mothers were given harmful drugs or those who were born by C-section.

All birth experiences are traumatic. The very act of going from the womb into independent life separate from the mother is essentially traumatic. Of course, most of us survive the journey, but the journey is nonetheless—and certainly to varying degrees—painful and disorienting. Life in the world will never be as satisfying as life in the womb where all of our needs are met.

For some of us, trauma began even in utero. Some mothers are alcoholics or on crack cocaine. Some are heroin addicts or prostitutes. Many are stressed out or emotionally/physically ill throughout their pregnancies.

There are wounds even in the womb, even in this place that is supposed to be completely safe. There are cracks in the protective armor from the very beginning.

If we emerge from the womb reasonably intact, we don't focus on any of this trauma. We just get on with it. Indeed, throughout our lives, as we go through one difficult transition after another, the expectation is "get on with it. Keep moving. Don't take it personally. That's life!"

I'm not saying that is a bad thing. We do have to get on with it. What I am trying to point out is that underneath the words "Get on with it" is a wounding experience that most of us stuff.

Both mother and baby stuff their pain. They will deal with it another time, or they won't.

Most of them don't deal with it.

When the birth experience is brutal, we take notice. We acknowledge the wound. When the mother tries to kill the baby, we pay attention. We know that child might have something to deal with later on.

But we all have something to deal with from the get-go. The wound is intricately woven in the tapestry of life. It is there at birth. It is there in childhood and puberty. It is there in adulthood and old age.

The birth of a sibling can be wounding. Having a friend beat you up can be wounding. Getting pregnant and having an abortion can be wounding. Breaking up with your spouse or leaving your children can be wounding. Having a spouse or a child get hurt, sick or die can be wounding.

Life is a chain of wounds. In between, all we can do is breathe!

I am not complaining or feeling sorry for us. I'm just observing. When we let go of our romantic interpretation of life and remove the sugar coating what we have is fairly primal.

Of course, we all try to find meaning in it, but the meaning may not be that there is something beside the wound—like beauty or love—to celebrate. It may be that the meaning is to be found in the wound itself.

As I have said previously, the wound is a tool of consciousness. It forces us to experience separation from self, from others and ultimately from our Source. Once we have experienced that separation, one of two things will happen. Either we will get depressed and give up or we will be determined to find connection.

Thanks to the wound, life is either a journey of alienation or a quest for connection. Often, it starts as the former and progresses to the latter. The moment when it shifts is usually a spiritual awakening experience.

Yes, we are the ones who give meaning to our lives, because we cannot accept the possibility that they could be without meaning. We cannot accept the possibility that the wound exists only to make us suffer.

The crazy thing is that if you do not give life this meaning, it will not have it. Nobody else is going to give it meaning for you. Nobody else is going to explain your wounds to you or justify them. Religion might try, but it fails miserably.

There is no justification for suffering. The wound is always painful. It is always terrible.

The question is not "Are we wounded?" (That is self-evident) or even "Why are we wounded?" (Not many care to know). The question is—and this has always been the question for human beings throughout the ages—what do you do with the wound? Can you heal it or will you pass it on?

If you do the former, you will pass the test of this embodiment. If you do the latter, you may have to come back and try again.

Once you heal the wound, you no longer have to experience it. But until then, you will feel its pain more and more deeply until it becomes unbearable. And that, for most of us, is the turning point.

That is when we step on the road to healing. That is when we give meaning to our lives and begin to take responsibility for the life that we are creating.

PARENTAL BETRAYAL

Separation creates the existential wound. It is a psychologically and emotionally painful event. Once we were connected to the whole and now we stand apart from it. We feel disoriented, lonely and alienated. We feel cut off from the Source that nurtures us, feeds us and holds us in her protective embrace.

Yet this is far more psychologically complex than we imagine, because the womb is not just the warm, fuzzy place that protects us, it is also the engine of our betrayal. The womb exists to give us birth. Its function is not just to hold us safe, but also to expel us from the kingdom. We look to Mommy as our savior, yet she is also the one who betrays us.

How is that for a set-up!

And Daddy has hardly a better rap. He is not only the creator, the one who seeds the womb, but also the one who cuts the umbilical cord. He is the one who takes us away from the mother, symbolically at birth, actually at puberty.

Daddy's sexuality, his desire, his hunger for the womb, can also be a wounding force, especially when his sexual energy is denied or pent up. Some Daddies rape and plunder. Some use their women as mere objects of their pleasure and imprison them, brutalize them, or abandon them. Some abuse their daughters and/or their sons.

Some Daddies are gentle, but many are not. Many are impatient, angry, even cruel.

Of course, you might have been one of the lucky ones. Daddy might have been kind to you and to your mom. He might have loved and cared for you, protected you, encouraged you to develop skill and confidence in your life. Daddy might have been your champion, your role model, and your guide.

But do not beat yourself up if he was not. Do not condemn yourself if neither Daddy nor Mommy knew how to show up for you. Don't be hard on yourself and don't be hard on them. Daddy's daddy didn't do any better by him. And Mommy's mommy was no pearl.

All of us live somewhere in the chain of abuse. That is just the way it is. Our pain may be moderate or it may be extreme, but all of us are in one kind of pain or another.

Remember, all this is a set up. You are wounded so that you will learn to heal yourself. You are rejected, abandoned, abused so that you will learn to love and accept yourself unconditionally.

That is the only reason you have come here.

Yes, of course, you must get on with it. That goes without saying. But first take note where it hurts. You will have to visit that place many times if you are going to find a way to heal your pain.

LOST INNOCENCE &
FRAGMENTATION OF SELF

When we are wounded, we lose touch with our innocence. When we are attacked, we assume that there is something bad about us. Why would anyone be mean to us if we were really *good*? It just doesn't compute. So we do the math ourselves. Being hurt = being bad. And that equation stays with us for a very long time. It forms the essence of our shame and our core belief about ourselves.

Once we accept the idea that we are bad, we have already accepted division in our psyche. Now part of us is bad and part of us is good. Part of us is dark and part of us is light. Part of us is shadow and part of us is persona.

The question we need to ask is "Where does our innocence go when we lose it?" For our innocence is not our persona, our light, or our goodness. Our innocence is an undivided state. Our innocence and our wholeness are one and the same.

Each of us is whole, innocent and free. Yet our psychological experience is that we feel divided; we feel guilty; we feel trapped in this body and this world. Some call this psychological state the dream or the illusion, and rightly so.

This is not our ultimate reality. It is not our true identify. It is just the way things feel and seem. It is just the psychological prison cell we inhabit.

The spiritual quest—the search for purpose and meaning—must be understood then as a journey to reclaim our lost innocence. It is a journey through the dualistic world in search of the original unity and oneness.

It is a journey through psychological pain into spiritual awareness, acceptance and bliss. It is a journey from separation to wholeness.

A Course in Miracles calls this a "journey without distance" because the place that we are traveling to is the place where we already are. We begin at the top of the circle and travel around the circle to the same place where we began, only now we see things differently. We see what we could not see before.

Our innocence was always there, but we could not see it. We had to make the journey to understand the place of our origin. We had to bring love to our fear, healing to our pain and forgiveness to our guilt to reclaim our innocence.

AMAZING GRACE

One of our most popular spiritual songs tells us: *I once was lost, but now I'm found. Was blind, but now I see.* These words accurately describe our spiritual awakening experience. We lose sight of our innocence and go searching for it as if it were the Holy Grail itself.

Each of us believes we are a "wretch," a sinner, a failure who needs to be saved. So we seek salvation out there in the world, but we do not find it.

Only Grace can save us. Because Grace tells us that our innocence was never lost. It was only forgotten and we can now remember it.

Once we were blindfolded and could not see the real meaning of things. Now, we have taken the blindfold off and we can see things as they truly are.

Truth is awakened when we are willing to see it. Until then, we will see only what we believe to be true, however erroneous that is.

Imagine this. *We come to this world merely to experience the limitations of what we believe.* We mistakenly believe that these limitations are real, but they are real only to the extent that we accept them. When we stop accepting untruth, it ceases to be true.

Illusions go when we stop holding them in place. Blindfolds have no power over us when we take them off.

Suffering seems to be very real, but it is real only because we have signed up to suffer. When we resign from the course, we don't have to go to class anymore.

I know a number of people who have taken *Crucifixion 101* at least six or seven times. As far as I know, Jesus took it only once and it was enough for him!

Yet people keep telling me "if it was good enough for Jesus, it's good enough for me" and they keep lining up at the door. You can always find a good preacher who is willing to teach that class.

Buddha, on the other hand, looked at suffering and concluded, "There is a way to put all this aside."

Now, if you take Buddha at his word, you can get off the cross and you don't have to get up on it anymore. You can be free of fear, anger, pain, and shame. You don't even have to meditate looking at a wall for 46 years.

Try to tell that to your Buddhist friends!

The truth is you don't have to meditate at all. You don't have to go to any classes. You don't have to go out like Don Quixote to find yourself or to save the world.

You just have to take that blindfold off. You just have to realize that what you believe about yourself and everybody else is not necessarily accurate or true.

What happens to the illusion when you stop holding onto it? It disappears, does it not?

That is why the greatest spiritual teachers tell you: Don't go in search of truth. That's a waste of time. Just let go of falsehood."

So many people think there is something specific here in the world for them to do. And they beat up themselves and everyone around them trying to do that thing.

However, this isn't really true. There is very little that we need to do here. The only thing we really need to do is to open our hearts to the power of love.

That's all. Nothing else is necessary.

We are here not so much to do, but to undo. We are here not to confirm our beliefs but to challenge them.

We are here not to suffer, but to free ourselves from suffering. On that topic, all the masters seem to agree.

PROMETHEUS

Prometheus was one of the Titans and he felt sorry for human beings. They were condemned to live in the cold, shivering and hungry. Their lives were truly miserable.

So Prometheus defied Zeus. He stole the fire from the gods and gave it to the humans so that they could stay warm and eat cooked food. Prometheus made human life bearable.

Prometheus gave humans the power of knowledge. He gave

them the capacity to understand and improve their lives. He gave them hope.

Without knowledge there is no hope. Knowledge is power.

In truth, we are here on Earth to learn how to love ourselves and how to love others. We do not know how to do this or we would not be here.

Earth is a school. The classes have been set up so that we are challenged from the start.

Of course, knowledge has a price. In our case, the price is the pain of the wound that helps us wake up. Prometheus, however, suffered an even worse fate. As punishment for his transgression, Zeus chained him to a rock where his liver was slowly consumed by an eagle. Each day the liver would grow back, because Titans were immortal, but each day it would be consumed again.

Knowledge is a gift that must be exercised every day. We can never be complacent with what we know. We owe Prometheus that.

Each of us bears a torch that will light our way home. It is up to us to gather up our light and tend to it so that it grows into a steady flame.

Each of us must understand the nature of our suffering and overcome it, so that we can light the way for others. Waking up is not just a solo act. Those who wake up hold the door open for others.

That is why every Buddhist nun or monk takes a vow not to enter Nirvana, the heavenly state, until all sentient beings are saved. They understand Prometheus' gift and know that it must be passed on.

PANDORA AND HER JAR

Yet another Greek Myth offers us insight into the nature of our awakening process. Pandora, whose name means "all gifted," was the first woman. She was created by Zeus and given gifts by all of the Gods. Hephaestus gave her form; Athena clothed her; Aphrodite gave her beauty; Apollo gave her musical talent and a gift for healing; Demeter taught her to tend a garden; Poseidon gave her a pearl necklace and the ability to never drown; Hera gave her curiosity; Hermes gave her cunning, boldness, and charm; Zeus gave her insatiable curiosity and mischievousness.

No one had more going for her than Pandora. However, we have to remember that Pandora was created by Zeus as part of the punishment of mankind for Prometheus' theft of the fire. Pandora was given a jar by Zeus and told never to open it. In that jar were all of the miseries that could beset humankind.

Well, you know the story. Pandora's curiosity was just too strong. She could not carry that jar around for very long without looking into it. So she tried to peak in, and out came all of the miseries of life. She closed the jar immediately, but it was too late. The only thing that she could keep in the jar was *hope.*

As long as *hope* remained in the jar, human life was filled with suffering. But then, one day, Pandora opened the jar again, and *hope* was released into the world. From that day onward, the human spirit was uplifted.

Prometheus' gift of fire (knowledge) and Pandora's gift of hope sustain us through all of our trials and travails. Because we carry these spiritual gifts, we can weather the storms of life. We can pass the tests and master the curriculum.

Like Pandora, we have many divinely inspired gifts to offer

the world. We are not just challenged. We are also blessed.

Indeed, one wonders if we would discover and value our gifts without the challenges of life that contrast so sharply with them, strengthening and preparing us to serve. Clearly, when we look back on our lives, we can see that all these challenges were necessary ingredients in our awakening.

Many of the people I meet are impatient. They want to serve right away. They want the fruit of the tree without tending to it: watering, weeding, and raking. However, the tree will not bear fruit if it is not cared for. Without our tending to the roots, there will be no fruit to harvest from the branches.

We must learn to be patient. We all come here with lessons to learn.

We cannot embody love until we learn to receive it. And we cannot receive it as long as we are running away in fear. We need to learn to stand our ground and tend our garden.

The spiritual path is not glamorous. It does not reward our egos. Indeed, the rewards are not short term—for there are no short cuts. They are long term. And those who are not patient and persistent do not experience the fruits of the journey.

WHAT'S REALLY IN THE JAR

I love the story of Pandora because it is such a set up. So was the story of Adam and Eve in the garden. Pandora was told, "No matter what, don't open that jar." Adam and Eve were told, "No matter what, do not eat the fruit of the Tree of Knowledge."

One thing that we know about human nature is that whenever we are told we cannot or should not do something, we will do it with a vengeance. Consider prohibition, for example. We outlawed alcohol and told people "You can't drink alcohol," and homemade stills started showing up in back yards all over the country.

Like I said, it is all a set up. And both these myths confirm that. Neither Pandora nor Adam and Eve had a chance.

Whatever we try to hide in the darkness of the psyche will surface sooner or later. There is simply no place to dump our stuff where it will disappear forever. No matter how good a stuffer you are, one day some guy with a shovel appears and starts uncovering it.

We want to have secrets, but life allows this only for a brief time. All secrets are bound to be revealed.

When we accept that, we realize that the jar is going to be opened. There is no stigma that should be attached to this. It is not Pandora's fault that she spilled the beans.

The beans are going to be spilled. Whatever happens in our lives must be dealt with, sooner or later.

Freud came up with the ingenious notion of an unconscious to help us understand our tendency to want to hide/deny the things that we cannot accept about ourselves or others. He wanted us to realize that there is a kingdom called SHAME. There is a place in consciousness where we bury our pain and cover up our wounds.

This place has been called many names. The Greeks called it the underworld. Freud called it the unconscious. It doesn't matter what you call it. It is the place that we are always trying to avoid. But no matter how hard we try, we cannot avoid it.

There is no way that you can escape your shadow self. If you don't visit it consciously, you will visit it in dreams. You will find a way to dialog with the disowned, repressed parts of yourself. Your healing—and the integration of your psyche—requires it.

So what exactly is in the jar that Pandora is carrying around? What are Adam and Eve hiding under those fig leaves?

They are hiding the creative essence of the universe. They are hiding the God-given power to create life, to create content and give it form.

Adam and Eve had two sons. One was called Able. The other was called Cain. Able represented all the good that they could create. Cain represented their capacity to create evil.

In other words, their creativity was a mixed bag (or a mixed jar if you prefer). They could create responsibly or irresponsibly. They could create that which nurtures and sustains life or that which injures and destroys it.

What are we really talking about here? Were not just talking about sexuality. That is far too narrow an understanding of what this means.

We are talking about free will. We are talking about choice. That's what lies under the fig leaf. That's the real issue hidden in the jar.

That's ironic, because we just pointed out that Pandora had no choice. She had to open the jar.

And what was in that jar? Another choice! And another. And another. What was in it? The whole karmic stream of events: all of our actions and reactions, all of our choices and their consequences.

No wonder it gets a little scary when the jar is opened.

We want to hide all this in the jar, but we can't. Life is an open book. Indeed, they say there is a record in the Ethers of everything that happens here: every choice, every thought, every feeling. There is nowhere for us to hide the contents of consciousness.

Einstein understood this better than Freud. He knew that inside the jar is an open field, a universal consciousness that is unfolding in all places at all times. We are part of that. Every decision that we make, every thought that moves through our mind is part of that.

What do you think Zeus put in that jar? What do you think God put in that apple?

It was no little thing when Prometheus stole the fire of the Gods. It was no little thing when Eve ate the apple.

Knowledge is power.

You and I have a choice. We can come to Earth and get lost in the dream. We can remain ignorant. Or we can wake up.

We can turn away from the torch, or we can learn to carry it. The choice is ours.

MENTORS AND GUIDES: MOVING INTO THE ARMS OF THE MOTHER

Before we choose to open the jar and look at what's inside, we have to learn to love and accept ourselves. We have to learn to hold all of the contents of our consciousness and experience in a compassionate way.

Otherwise, we will go crazy when we look in the jar. We will be overwhelmed with the contents. Our psychiatric institutions are filled with people who tried to face their fears before they were ready.

So the first practice that we do is to learn to hold our fears with compassion. We learn to accept our mistakes and to forgive our trespasses. We see how hard we can be on ourselves and we learn to be more gentle with ourselves.

When fear comes up, instead of stuffing it or pushing it away, we learn to hold it gently. We learn to bring acceptance and love to our experience moment to moment.

When we have learned to do this, we can open the jar with immunity. We can feel the hurts and wounds that lurk underneath our fears with compassion for ourselves. We can begin to unpeel the onion of our pain and take the journey into the depths of the underworld.

Some try to take the journey alone, but I do not advise it. It is better to go with a mentor or a guide who knows the territory. Whether your guide is a friend or a therapist, she must have experienced her own dark night of the soul. She must have felt her pain and healed her anger and her grief.

She must have no agenda or ax to grind or she will be unable to help you. Only one who has visited the deepest and darkest crannies of her heart can guide you through those scary places in your own.

So choose your guide carefully. Look for the fruits of integration and empowerment in her life. Then, get to know and trust each other. It is unwise to take the journey without a guide you can trust.

Check in with your guide at least once per week. If possible have the support of a loving community.

Make sure that there are people you can call when you get scared or overwhelmed, people who will hold the rope for you when you need to climb out of some cave full of monsters or demons.

It takes courage to look at your shadowy material. It is never a pretty site and there's always the risk that you will believe that it is really your identity.

It isn't, but sometimes it doesn't seem that way. There are times when you are exploring the hurt places in your heart and it hurts so much it seems that there is no hope of relief.

When you lose sight of the light, you need to take out your candle and light it. And, if you forgot to bring the candle or the flashlight, you can borrow one from your guide. A good guide always carries the light when she goes into the darkness.

One needs to be prepared. One must know the territory.

Your guide and your community are not directing you so much as they are just holding the space for your healing. They are standing by to help out in case you get lost or disoriented.

They are available to hold you when you need to curl up into a fetal position and begin to sob. They are there to love you when you forget how to love yourself.

Your spiritual family/community holds the Mother energy for you as you allow the False Self to crumble. It witnesses the death of your ego consciousness and your rebirth in Spirit. It holds the doorway open to you as you move out of victimhood into your full empowerment as a human being.

Your birth mother was not able to give you unconditional love and acceptance, but now you have a Mother who can do so. The Community embraces you unconditionally. It sees you though the birth canal and welcomes you on the other side. It does not abandon you.

This is the true Mother you need. In her arms you are healed.

And then you become the Mother. You become the one who holds the space of unconditional love and acceptance for others.

When we have healed, our wound of abandonment disappears. We know that we cannot ever be abandoned, because we cannot abandon ourselves.

That is Divine Mother's gift to us. She teaches us how to love ourselves without conditions.

PART 7

Recovering Our Innocence

*Our spirituality is a courageous quest
to reclaim our lost innocence.*

*It is a journey through psychological pain
into spiritual awareness, acceptance and bliss.
It is a journey from separation to wholeness.*

Beverly's Story

I met Beverly for the first time some fifteen years ago. She attended a workshop I gave in Charlottesville, Virginia. Years later, she shared with me that this workshop had been a turning point in her life. I did not know her story then, nor did I see her for many years. But when I put out the call to my readers to come and do the deep emotional healing work, Beverly was one of the first people to show up.

The work asked Beverly to revisit many of the hurt places inside her heart. This wasn't an easy thing to do, as you will see when you hear her story, nor was it the first time that Beverly had taken that journey. Yet, in spite of her courage in dealing with her wounds in therapy, something was missing in Beverly's healing process. After a while, it became clear to me. Beverly had moved through layers of healing and forgiveness, but she had not been fully empowered. She did not fully trust her healing and she was not reaching out to help others in the way that I knew she could.

I kept inviting Beverly to step forward and become a leader and a role model for the younger women in our community, particularly those who had been abandoned and/or sexually abused as children. It took a while. Something kept holding her back. Perhaps it was the fear that in stepping forward to help others, she would be constantly recycling the pain of her wound. Actually, it would be quite the opposite.

By being a witness for others, she would detach from her own drama and surrender to deeper layers of love, acceptance and forgiveness. In helping others to heal, she would be able to go through the final stages of her own healing process. And then she would come into her power as the wise woman, spiritual guide and healer that she was meant to be. Here's her story:

I first met Paul Ferrini in the early 1990s. By that time I had been married, raised four children badly, and had been severely depressed and suicidal. To understand why, it might be helpful for me to share with you some of the details of my earlier life.

I was born illegitimate as the result of date rape, I am told. When I was born there was a state law that out of wedlock babies must have ILLEGITIMATE stamped on their birth certificates. Marked second class from birth, I carried that feeling through most of my life.

My mother emotionally abandoned me at six weeks. She became a wet nurse for a wealthy doctor's family and I was put in a crib on a bottle. We lived very well in a large house with servants but as I grew up no one told me that the family was not my family. The man that I called Daddy was not my Daddy, nor were my two sisters and brother my siblings by birth.

As I look back, I see that I was treated more like a pet than a child. Each morning my mother would get me up and, as soon as I could crawl, I bounced down the back stairs on my bum and went to the kitchen to see Cook and George (the driver). They acted like they thought I was as special as I did. Smiles, hugs and special treats were in the kitchen for me every morning. This was my first experience of unconditional love and the last for a very long time.

My real grandmother came on a Greyhound bus and took me home with her when I was 18 months old, after I had been told that my coughing was keeping the entire family awake and Doctor needed his sleep. So I had to go. We left on a bus. As we walked to the bus stop I was so scared I had an out of body experience. I saw the entire scene with my mother, grandmother and me from across the street and from behind.

We went to the back seat of the bus so I could see my mother. I saw her getting smaller and smaller and when the bus turned the corner I could not see her anymore. I lay down on the seat facing the back and a part of me died that day. The shock and trauma was so severe to me that I stayed out of body for some time. I was in a world where I knew no one and no one seemed to like me much.

Their dislike for me grew after my uncle Butler raped me under the house when I was four. Just what do you do when your son rapes your illegitimate grand daughter? You tell no one, put her to bed and dope her up. I was conscious of nothing for a good long time. It was summer when I was raped and the next thing I remember was seeing myself, again from the back, walking up the porch steps in a snowsuit.

This child was wounded so deeply that she did not even begin to recover for 51 years. I grew up a disintegrated personality trying to cope (living was not an option) in a world where no one seemed to want me and everything seemed to be my fault.

I lived with my grandmother until I was seven. During that time my mother came to see me once and I was taken to see her twice. When I was six my grandmother and I made a trip by train to Ohio to see two of her sons, my uncles. We stayed in a big farm-house in the middle of acres and acres of flowers.

My uncles were in the commercial flower growing business. There was a small store across the highway where one of my uncles would take me every few days for ice cream. On this day my grandmother said that she would take me, but when we got to the front of the lawn she decided that she would watch me from there. There was a ten-mile an hour speed limit in front of the store. Off I went with my five pennies.

As I crossed the road I heard my grandmother scream and I turned and was hit by a speeding car. The car skidded 350 feet before coming to a halt and I fell off the bumper and lay face down in the highway. I could see people coming from the house but they were coming so slow, like in a dream. I looked down the road in the opposite direction and there was another car speeding toward me and I knew that my family would never get there in time. The driver saw the accident and stopped.

When I began to work with my traumas these were the worst feelings to deal with: helplessness and abandonment.

Anyway, I lived, although there was some doubt about that for the first 24 hours. I didn't know that, because I was out like a light with a broken pelvis, punctured liver, bleeding spleen, serious abrasions on both feet. I was in a cast from under my arms to my ankles for over two months, July and August. After learning to walk again, I returned to my grandmother's home for a few months.

Then my mother married and I moved to Memphis to live with her and my stepfather. That is another story.

Even though I was seven, I had to wait until the next fall to enter public school so I attended an Episcopal school for the rest of that year. What a blessing that was. Although I was poor and not an Episcopalian, I found a place there and hated it when I had to leave. There I was not illegitimate. I was Beverly Jean and I was smart, learned quickly and had a talent for dance. It was a world I could not even have dreamed of.

That summer my stepfather was bedridden with a heart problem and each day I had to stay with him for at least two hours (I hated it). He would read me stories and he read well with a lot of drama and kept me interested. One day he started rubbing his fingers on the elastic on my panties. I didn't know what to do, so I just lay there as if nothing was happening. When he started to put his fingers inside my pants, I jumped up and ran across the room. He kept saying "come back, I won't do that anymore" but I would not.

I never spent any time with him alone after that until my teens and he never said a thing. When I was sixteen, he started exposing himself to me whenever my mother wasn't home. By that time I was smarter and avoided him after the first time.

I won a scholarship to a college in Missouri but I had to go to the campus to meet with the dean before it was official. Mother told me that we didn't have the money for the trip and then went out and bought a new suit. I didn't feel worthless. I felt non-existent.

I had four different personalities . . . my way of coping, I guess. I remember two of them (the other two were minor). I was the church lad: prim, stiff, trying to be perfect. Then I was the harlot, who used sex as a weapon, as an enticement or reward for getting what she wanted.

When the birth control pill came out, I wondered if I was true to my husband because I wanted to be or because I was afraid not to be. I found out several months later after we had moved to Europe for my husband's job and I had my first affair. Now, I had the power and it felt good.

It felt good until I started to fall apart emotionally. I had been on medication off and on since my middle twenties. This time nothing helped. I called my Ob-Gyn one afternoon, in a very bad way, thinking it was hormonal. By six o'clock that evening I was in an institution on suicide watch every ten minutes. If you have never *heard the sound of a steel door of a psychiatric hospital close behind you, you do not truly understand the word "hopeless."*

I had been there five weeks when another bomb hit. My blood test showed that I might have Chronic Leukemia. I was there another seven weeks while they searched for T cells and B cells and counted lymphs and platelets. Finally I went home.

My husband and I had separated and I had bought a log cabin in the middle of a national forest. I had two dogs for company but the night I went home to the cabin they were still in a kennel. So I went home alone, threw my suitcase down and went up to the loft to bed. Sometime later I was awakened by a very bright light. It looked rather like a Jacob's ladder from physics. It was, kind of. It was an electrical fire and my cabin was burning.

This was in December in the mountains of Virginia and it was eight degrees. My portable phones didn't work and I was heavily medicated. I picked up my bag and keys and drove down the lane until I found a house with lights on. No one was home but I went in to call the fire department.

This was a blazing homecoming from the nut house. I lived in an apartment for a year while my cabin was rebuilt. I really learned nothing about myself in the hospital so I went to a psychiatrist and then to a social worker with whom I worked for nearly three years. In the meantime, I did 21 rebirthing hours and got involved in a psychic development group led by David McKnight who became my spiritual teacher for some years to come.

After that, Paul Ferrini made a stop in Charlottesville on his way to New Mexico and I had the opportunity to meet him and spend an evening in his energy and listen to him speak. I have never forgotten that night. I have held the desire in my heart to be able to have that kind of energy for myself. I am still working on it. I read everything Paul had written and it was like angel wings against my soul. I made more progress with my new counselor and began to have a little more confidence in my own ability to live closer to the present than the past. We decided it would be a good idea for me to attend an Incest Survivor's weekend because of my stepfather.

The things I heard that weekend made my blood run cold. Satanic ritual abuse starting very young and lasting for years, parents prostituting young girls, fathers having intercourse with their daughters with the mothers watching, mothers sexually abusing their daughters, you name it. This retreat was for females so we didn't hear of the boys' abuse. Still, the only thing that seemed to hit me was when a girl talked about blood on her underwear. I felt that somewhere down inside.

Three weeks later I was skiing with a friend in West Virginia. It was a Thursday. I had skied about an hour and suddenly there I was at the top of a diamond and could not do anything right. I basically couldn't ski. My friend thought I had gone nuts and so did I. My body would do nothing I gave it the command to do. I am a good skier but not that day. It took me forty-five minutes to get down a slope I did in fifteen with ease. At the bottom of the slope, I told my friend that I was going in the lounge for a while and would pick him up in a few minutes.

As I turned to go in the lounge, I thought I saw a little girl lying in the snow on her left side. I said to myself "you are nuts." When I came back out there she was again-- only this time she was facing me. The question came, "Is that me?" I put the whole thing out of my mind and skied rather badly the rest of the day.

The next morning the rape memory returned in a blaze of pictures and words. I got a legal pad and started writing down the words and describing the pictures. I wrote for hours, thinking the entire time, "This is not true; I am making this up." The words and pictures kept coming and I kept writing until I was exhausted.

I called some of my aunts who had lived in the house and every detail checked out. They even added some things that happened after the rape that I didn't know.

I cried and cried and even rented a sad movie so I would not stop crying. I kept at it until I felt empty. Then I got mad. Rage at my abuser, who had been my favorite uncle. If he hadn't already been dead, I would have killed him, and gladly gone to jail.

I still had a baby doll that was named after the two of us. I called her Beverly-Butts, and I loved her. I loved her until then. In my anger I took that doll and smashed her head against the brick fireplace and pieces flew everywhere. I picked up the pieces and smashed them again with the poker. The body was cloth so I stabbed and ripped that into pieces. I started a fire in the wood stove and put the pieces in it and burned them.

I had heard that ashes were good for fruit trees. So after the stove cooled, I took the ashes and spread them around a peach tree in the back yard. The next spring the tree died.

What can I tell you? Rage is a mighty thing. It kills. It had been killing me for years.

The memories continued to come up for several years but, as I began to heal and connect with myself and that little girl, they didn't hurt anymore. I finally forgave my uncle after having a better understanding of his pain. The forgiving was for me, not him. Hopefully, God had already forgiven him.

I attended my first retreat with Paul in December of 2004. Attending this retreat was a little scary for me, but I knew that I needed to go. Being there was an experience like no other. There I found the family I had never had and I experienced unconditional love from Paul and from the other Mastery students.

A lot of my journey on the path has been taken alone. Not so anymore! Now I am surrounded by a loving community of sisters and brothers. Each one is a light and an inspiration in my life.

Since I have joined the community I have been sharing my journey of healing from childhood sexual abuse with other women who have similar experiences. As Paul says in his books, the wound and the gift are intricately related. As I heal my wound, I can help others heal.

I know that I could have saved myself many years of torture if I had found this kind of help, as well as the support of a loving community, earlier on in my healing process. My hope is that I can save others some of the torture that I went through and help them reclaim their beauty, their power and their innocence!

Beverly's story gives us hope that we can heal from any kind of trauma if we are willing and we have enough support. Thanks to her and other courageous members of our community who are willing to share their healing journeys, people are able to heal their trauma earlier on in their lives and in a fraction of the time it would otherwise take.

HEALING INTO MASTERY AND SERVICE

When Beverly moved from Level One to Level Two of our Spiritual Mastery Program, I asked her to clarify some of the issues related to her healing. The following dialog took place:

Paul: Beverly, what do you see as your core wound?

Beverly: I have two core wounds.

The first was being emotionally abandoned from birth. I was not loved or wanted. As a child of "date rape," I was the cause of my mother's unhappiness. I was held responsible for everything that happened to my mother from the time I was born.

I was an object, an IT, not a person. I was always on my guard not to do anything that would embarrass my mother.

Not having a soft place to fall as a child made me tense, shy, and scared all the time, waiting for the next shoe to fall. I developed a fight or flight response that became molecular and defined my life.

My second core wound was being raped by my uncle when I was four. He was the one person that I thought loved me. So much for trust and love.

Paul: How did therapy help you deal with these wounds?

Beverly: The first thing that I had to deal with was my mother wound. I remember that my mother used to write me such horrible letters that I have almost fainted at the mailbox. I went to a psychiatrist who taught me how to deal with her letters. That was step one out of my hole.

Then, I began therapy with a clinical social worker. I was with her every week for four years. That helped me put myself in a safe place so that I could begin to get out from the load of shame that I was carrying. However, I knew while I was in the hospital that I needed to change therapists.

My next therapist was Mary, a much gentler and more spiritual person. We were together a year and a half before she guided me to the sexual abuse weekend led by Kate Hutchens. Through this work the memory of my rape returned.

Previously, the hidden sexual abuse drove my life. The memory brought all this out in the open so that I could deal with it. By that time I had grown as a person and I had had a number of insights. I was no longer living as a victim.

Paul: What were some of things you learned about sexual abuse?

Beverly: Any child that has been sexually abused develops ways to hide the shame. We become carnal before our time, confuse sex and love and understand neither. We act out sexually and sex becomes a tool for power. Every time we use (misuse) sex our guilt gets heavier and our shame grows and we diminish a bit more.

Paul: How have you shared your insights in the program?

Beverly: Facilitating the *Affinity Process* for other women who have been sexually abused has been powerful for me. At my first retreat, my fear of my age setting me apart from others and feeling like an odd ball was quickly erased when I decided to let go of my fear and open up.

Also, another level of healing opened up for me when I told my story in the telephone sexual support group to people I had never met. That, along with facilitating support groups at retreats, has steadily given me more courage and self-confidence. The Mastery Program has supported me in stepping into a leadership role as I have felt ready to do so.

Paul: What are the gifts that you bring to this work?

Beverly: I have an open and empathetic heart. I can feel the discomfort of others and can help them to release the pain they are holding onto. I am a good and active listener. I read energy so I can tell when some one is doing the "shuck and jive." I have a pretty good sense of humor that can be used to lighten a heavy atmosphere. I love.

There are many motherless women in the world that need a

loving, empathetic mentor who has been there and knows the way. I have been working with four such women during the past five years. They have all graduated now and are flying high in their own power.

I am also very sensitive to the specific needs of women who have been sexually abused. It is clearly one of my *Houses of Healing*. Sexual abuse is like an illness that no one knows that you have and you are afraid to tell. Once you tell, it opens up a new wasp nest that may hurt you and the people involved. You have to tread gently.

Paul: Where are the places in your body where you consistently feel energy, especially at retreats and when doing spiritual work?

Beverly: I consistently feel energy in my heart and in my hands. I may also feel it on my face and head and shoulders. During guided meditations I feel it everywhere. My skin tingles all over, all of my chakras feel energized and energy flows down my front and around and up the back. In doing Reiki, I feel energy in my heart, hands and face. I am a second level Reiki practitioner. I do not do Reiki for money. I do it to help those who need it.

Paul: As you know, the more we open to our own healing, the more we are able to embody the energy of unconditional love.

It becomes a palpable presence in our heart, our hands, our feet, our head, indeed in every cell of our body. We vibrate with the energy of love and it spontaneously flows through us to others.

This is a natural result of our work in the Program.

BERNARD'S STORY

Like Beverly, Bernard came to the first three Mastery retreats. These retreats happened over a four-month period and provided an intensive experience of what I call "the container" energy of unconditional love and acceptance.

During the retreats, people drop their masks and get real with each other. They explore their fear, their pain, their shame, their grief and anything else that might be up. All this is done is a very safe environment where participants feel loved and accepted.

Living in this energetic embrace for several days, our defense mechanisms (the ways that we push love away) are exposed and our self-betrayal becomes transparent. We learn to accept the love that is there for us and to honor the True Self that is waiting to be born.

For Bernie, the wound was a deep one. But most of his recent pain was centered on being in a job that he did not want to do. He dreaded going to work and felt a tremendous inner pressure to quit. However, he stayed in the job for security reasons. The longer he stayed, the sharper the pain and the self-betrayal became.

To understand what was behind that pain and self-betrayal, you have to know Bernie's story. Here is it is his words:

About two months before I was born my abusive father beat my mother up pretty badly. He was insanely jealous and full of rage and told my mother that he didn't believe that I was his child. During the beating he kicked my mother in the stomach and did some real damage. As a result, she hemorrhaged and died on the table when she was giving birth to me. It was not her fault, but I was abandoned at birth and left to live with my angry alcoholic father.

My father had been in World War Two and was living on disability. I am sure that he had his own wounds and demons, but I never really got to know him. I was the last of eleven children and all of the boys had been physically abused by him. Of course, I was just a baby and I don't remember any of this, but I know from my siblings that he used to tie me up by my arms and my legs inside my crib. I slept in an unheated attic room that was so cold there were literally icicles dripping down from the ceiling.

Fortunately, I was not with my birth father very long. Six months after I was born, one of my aunts reported my father to social services and I was taken from the house the day after Christmas. I was subsequently adopted by a new family.

I was in the hospital for three months after that with pneumonia and I almost died. Nine months later my life changed again when the couple that adopted me decided to get divorced. Fortunately, I stayed with my mother, who subsequently remarried, and for four years things were somewhat stable in my life.

Now, I know that this woman wasn't my real mother any more than my stepfather was my real father, but she was the closest thing to a mother that I had. Even though she was very sickly during those years—constantly coughing and getting around in a wheelchair—she was kind to me. And I guess I bonded with her. I remember that she would send me out to pick dandelions and then she would make me a necklace out of them.

Consistent motherly love was evidently not in the cards for me, because when I was six, my mother died of cancer. She had been in the hospital several times and I remember visiting her there. But then one day, she just died, and I watched as they came to the house to take her away.

So I guess you can say I was abandoned twice: once by my real mother at birth, and again six years later by my adopted mother. You can see that this is a core wound for me. Of course, it wasn't their fault that they died. Neither one of them deliberately abandoned me, but it was abandonment nonetheless.

I was now living with Sam, my third father. He and my mother had adopted another child after I came to live with them, so he was left with me and my sister, plus two teenage girls that my mother had had in a previous marriage. He was a decent man, but he was not looking forward to bringing up four kids by himself, so he immediately remarried.

That's when Maggie, my third mother, showed up in my life. She brought with her three children from her previous marriage, so there were seven of us. Well, Maggie and I never got along. In fact, it seemed like she had it out for me from the beginning. She used to hit my younger sister and me quite often and she was always trying to get rid of us so that she could have Sam to herself. Once she forced me to take a bunch of tests in the hope that she would be able to prove that I was retarded and get me sent away to a state home.

There was a real double standard in the family. Maggie treated her kids one way, and my sister and me another. We were clearly second-class citizens. No only that, but her two boys were always ganging up on me. I spent the next eight years literally fighting them both off. I learned to be tough so that I could survive.

Sam and Maggie were dysfunctional. Sam was an alcoholic and a workaholic. He basically just dumped the kids on Maggie and avoided everything. Maggie was an unhappy woman who took out her frustrations on us. Both of them were having affairs throughout the marriage. One day, all the issues in the family came to a head.

I remember this vividly, because it seems to sum up how alone, rejected and angry I felt growing up. Several of my friends were coming over to my house to pick me up so that we could go to school to take our history final. Maggie was slapping me around, as she frequently did, and I was standing in the kitchen, holding my arms up to fend off her attack. Then, out of the corner of my eye, I noticed my friends watching all this outside the screen door and I felt such rage and humiliation. I just snapped. I picked Maggie up and threw her over the dining room table, screaming, "You'll never touch me again, Bitch!"

I left the house, went to take my history final, and then went out into the woods, hiking along the Erie Canal. Nature was my only solace growing up. It was the only place where I felt peaceful and nurtured. That, I suppose, is one of the great gifts that I was given in my life. My love of the outdoors has helped me to heal and I know that it is a gift that I can share with others.

Anyway, when Sam found out what had happened he told me, "Don't worry about her. By this weekend, we will have her out of the house." And he kicked her and her children out. But then when we were moving some things from the house to her new apartment, we caught Maggie on top of her oldest son—a fourteen-year-old boy—having sex with him. She had been abusing him and he was the glory boy, the beautiful one who did everything right. She always compared me to him; I was the black sheep who was ugly and couldn't do anything right. But look what she did to him! After he left high school, he never spoke to her again.

My high school years were fairly stable. Sam left money on the table and I would go shopping and cook for my sister and myself. But I also started to get involved with drugs and alcohol then. I would smoke pot every day and drink on the weekends. Needless to say, I didn't do very well in school. I failed a number of classes and, if it weren't for summer school, I would not have made it through high school.

Eventually Sam found himself another woman, but this one

wasn't much older than I was. She was only twenty-one and he got her pregnant. So, during my senior year in high school, she moved in with us and had her baby.

Around that time, I fell in love with the girl that I was dating, but I couldn't see staying around my hometown. I felt there had to be more to life than getting married and having children. So I enlisted in the military. This broke my girlfriend's heart and it was to be the first of many betrayals.

In the military, I was very promiscuous and slept with every woman who was willing to give me time and attention. Yet at the same time, I continued to keep my relationship going with my girlfriend back home. I kept telling her that I loved her and wanted to marry her, even though it was obvious that I couldn't be faithful to her.

Later, I married my girlfriend and had two children with her. But my pattern of promiscuity—with the resulting lies, deceptions and attempts to cover up—continued. The truth was I just did not know how to be committed to anyone, even to myself.

It took me a while to understand my reactive behavior pattern. On the one hand, I was driven to seek the company of women, searching for the love I had never received from my mothers. Yet, at the same time, since consistent, committed love had never been modeled for me, I was unable to be committed to any of these women. As a result, I became the one who betrayed and abandoned others.

One core belief I had about myself was that I was an ugly duckling. This was Maggie's constant message to me and I internalized it at a very deep level. My reactive behavior pattern was to try to prove her wrong by adding as many notches to my belt as possible. The more women who fell for me, the less ugly I felt.

My wife loved me and I loved her. My affairs were never about love. They were always about sex, which for me was some form of validation that I craved. That's because there was a gaping hole in my heart. No matter how much I fed that hole with my sex addiction, it felt empty and unsatisfied.

Of course, it wasn't sex that I wanted. I wanted love, but I did not know how to give it or receive it.

Meanwhile I was feeling guilty about deceiving my wife, but I could not bring myself to tell her the truth. We began to drift apart and I became more and more depressed. In the end, I decided to end the marriage, even though I had promised myself that I would never do that to my children. I left the marriage without having dealt with any of my issues.

Dealing with the pain of leaving my marriage helped me begin to look at myself. But that process intensified greatly when I met Rachael. My relationship with her was to be a real turning point for me. For the first time in my life I was completely honest with the woman I was with. I told her about my history of infidelity and she confided in me about her own destructive patterns. She really forced me to look at myself. We had no secrets from each other. And, for the first time in my life, I was completely faithful.

A lot began to shift in my life around this time. On my fortieth birthday, I woke up and it was a beautiful, sunny day and I decided to climb a mountain in the Adirondacks and sat up on this mountaintop for three hours and began to acknowledge my birth mother. Through my tears, I carried on a conversation with her and was able to connect with her on a profound level. Later, I realized that she died at age forty, my present age. Something had come full circle for me.

My relationship with Rachael brought many gifts to me. Rachael and I read Love Without Conditions together and she strongly supported my interest in spirituality. It was through her urging and *support that I decided to attend Paul Ferrini's first Mastery retreat. That was when my healing journey took a leap forward and I was able to share my shame and my pain with others. The more I shared, the more the pain and shame began to lift.*

I began to understand my core wound and to meet others in the community who had the same wound. I saw clearly how I was living a lie in order to win the approval of others and I didn't want to do that anymore. I decided to risk being myself and to quit the job that I hated. I sold my house and simplified my life.

I let my False Self crash without trying to pick up the pieces. And I began to trust my True Self. Since that time, I have hardly looked back. One door has opened after another and I have walked through each one. Of course, it wasn't always the door that I expected to open. But I have learned to put my expectations aside so I can flow with what is unfolding. This allows me to live more in the present moment, to surrender and to trust.

After many years of depression, joy has come back into my life. I am no longer living to win approval or prove my worthiness. I am content to be who I am and to be honest with others about that.

My mask has come off. A huge burden has been lifted from me.

Several years ago I would not have been able to live in this surrendered way. I would have agonized over "not knowing." I would have demanded that I have a plan for my life so that I could feel secure. Now I know that this kind of security does not exist. And the attempt to find it is tantamount to building a prison around yourself. I can't do that anymore.

As a baby I was tied down in my crib. I was literally imprisoned. Later, I created a prison for myself trying to win the love and approval of others. I can't do that anymore. I have to be authentic, even if others do not understand.

Fortunately, as I have learned to accept myself and move into my healing, I have begun to attract people into my life who love and accept me without conditions. My relationship with Rachael and the love and acceptance of the Mastery community have played a big role in birthing me into my new life.

To put it simply, my life is not the same. I am a changed person. I have healed the major portion of my mother wound.

I no longer feel betrayed or abandoned, because I have learned to show up for myself and the people I care about. I don't have to run away from love any more. I don't have to be unfaithful to others, or to myself. My reactive behavior patterns no longer run my life.

My journey of healing tells me one thing loud and clear: If I can heal, you can heal. Healing is possible for all of us who are willing. Love is more powerful than we can imagine. When we have the courage to open our hearts and invite love in, it transforms every aspect of our lives. I am living proof of that.

HEALING THE WOUND, FINDING THE GIFT

The Mastery program gave Bernie the tools and the confidence he needed to step forward as a facilitator of healing for others. His *Laws of Love* classes in the Albany/Sarasota, New York area have opened doors for others seeking healing and empowerment.

For some time I have felt that Bernie's *House of Healing* had something to do with helping kids who have been abandoned or abused, or who come from broken homes. That's because no one better understands these kids and the challenges that they face than Bernie. He has walked in their moccasins. That gives him insight and credibility.

One of Bernie's gifts is an understanding and appreciation

of nature. He enjoys taking people out into the wilderness on vision quests and helping them experience the healing power of nature. I have always seen him doing this with abused children and teenagers. Bernie is very receptive to this, but he also feels that he wants his work to be Spirit-driven. He no longer wants to try and make it happen through his ego structure.

Recently, Bernie shared with me that the Director of Foster Care services for his area is one of the students in his current *Laws of Love* class. I doubt this is a coincidence. Indeed, I am always amazed at the power of Spirit and how it works in our lives. Yet I also know that we can't make anything happen. So I appreciate the humility and surrender in Bernie's words when he says: "I don't know what this means, but I plan to show up and see what happens."

After you do this work for a while, you realize that complete surrender is what is required. You can't figure it out in your head. You just have to open your heart and be present. You can't make the mistake of thinking that *you* are doing it. You just have to let it be done through you.

Each of us is asked to get out of the way and let Spirit work through us. That is how our gift can best be utilized. If we try to take charge or be in control, we will limit our gift or its expression.

We have to remember that we are not the ones who help or heal. Love does it through us. Each of us is merely an instrument of God's abundance and grace.

God does not ask us for much. S/he asks only for our willingness, but that is enough. That is what creates the pathway for the expression of love in the world.

LOVE IS THE GREATEST GIFT

I tell the Mastery students that the only real gift is the gift of love. And you cannot give this gift until you receive it.

Bernie could not show up for others until he learned to show up for himself. If you ask him the most important thing that he has learned in the Mastery program and in his life, he would tell you without hesitating "I learned to love myself."

That is the foundation of our spiritual work. We cannot help others heal until we can say from the depths of our hearts "I really love myself." Because that is what we are asked to model.

To truly love ourselves, we must drop our masks and address our wounds. We must see our suffering and our reactive behavior patterns and look behind them to find out where it really hurts. We must come to terms with our Core Wound and our Core Belief about ourselves.

What do we build as long as we are unconsciously driven by our wounds? We build the False Self. And the False Self becomes our prison. It keeps our pain locked in.

Sooner or later, if we want to be happy, we have to dissolve the walls of that prison. We have to liberate the True Self. And there is only one way to do it.

We have to bring love to the wounded parts of ourselves. When we bring love, our wounds heal. Our reactive behavior patterns end. We stop betraying ourselves.

That is when we become authentic and step into our power. That is when we wake up.

Only one who has learned to bring love to the wound can

heal and be empowered. Only one who has wrapped her arms around the shadow and invited the wounded child to sit on her lap can heal the pain of that child.

There are many wounded children in this world walking around in adult bodies. They trespass on each other. They attack and defend. They trigger the wound over and over again.

All the brutality of human life is directly connected to our core wounds. This brutality—indeed the whole cycle of violence—will not end until each of us has the courage to face our wound and heal it.

Lest we look within, we will continue to be a victim or a victimizer. If you look around, that is what you will see in this world. Some do a better job of disguising their pain than others, but peel back the onion, look behind the mask and you will see the demons that lurk in every mind and every heart.

We all have a choice in this life. We can learn to bring love or we can refuse to do it.

If we learn to bring love, we will move out of victimhood. We will step into our power and become authentic. This very act empowers others and models the work of healing and transformation for them. We don't have to have a formal role in their lives. Our mere presence in their lives is transformational.

Just by showing up and being who he is, Bernie is a witness to the power of love. He radiates the presence of love because it has taken root in his heart.

We all have many gifts. Bernie has the gift of being a guide in nature. Carolina has the gift of painting. Ella has the gift of making collage. Sharing these gifts brings the most profound joy.

But we have to remember that the only gift that we can ever give or receive is the Gift of Love. All other gifts are different forms of this one.

Bernie told me recently, "I can't be around anyone any more without telling them that I love them. I know that is because I have learned to love myself.

Today that love is there for everyone. Even when people are being difficult, I know that it is just because they are wounded and feel cut off from the Source. So I can look past their behavior. I can reach out to the hurt little kid in them just as I have learned to reach out to my own."

PART 8

The Law of Attraction

Until we heal our wounds we will create suffering.
It's that simple.

Only the True Self can create something of value
to ourselves or to others.

Attraction and Detraction

Today there is a great deal of buzz about the Law of Attraction. Unfortunately, few people understand this law at depth and a superficial understanding of this law often causes more harm than good. Instead of helping people manifest their dreams, an incomplete understanding of how this law works results in our repeated self-betrayal and failure. This reinforces our shame and powerlessness.

Why do we try to manifest our dreams and fail? Because we are creating from our wound, not from our Core Self. Until we heal our wounds, we cannot manifest our gift or give it to others. Until we heal our pain, all we will do is recreate it over and over again. Needless to say this can be very frustrating.

Until we heal our wounds and find out who we are and what we really want, we are going to create suffering. It's that simple. The False Self can manifest only its own illusions.

When our ego gets hold of the Law of Attraction—and that's what usually happens—it goes crazy. Not only does it begin building a bigger and better rocketship to heaven, but it also decides to invest its life savings in the plan. When the rocketship crashes, the ego often crashes with it.

Sometimes it gets pretty messy. It can even seem catastrophic, but actually it is a good thing. The ego must die if the True Self is to be born. Only the True Self understands and abides by the principles of this law.

For most of us, the Law of Attraction quickly turns into the Law of Detraction. It is yet another concept that we use to try to skip the inevitable baby steps we need to take on the spiritual path.

Instead of trying to blast off into our abundance, we need to learn to put one foot in front of the other. I know that isn't very glamorous, but it is the only thing that works.

We don't need motors to climb the mountain. We need strong muscles.

HOW THIS LAW REALLY WORKS

For the Law of Attraction to work, you must create through your connection with your Core Self. That means that you are creating out of the awareness that you are loved and you are worthy.

If you do not have a connection with your Core Self, you cannot create anything of value.

In addition you must know what you really want. If the False Self is still running your life, then you are still trying to please others, so you cannot know what you really want. All you know is what others want for you.

That is why I tell the Mastery Students, "As long as the False Self is in charge, you would be wise "to refrain from creating" because you aren't going to like what you create. You will not be creating for your highest good or the highest good of others.

Only through the connection to our Core Self can we understand who we really are and what we really want. So creating that connection must be step one in the manifestation process. Everything else depends on it.

As we establish the connection to our Core Self, old patterns of self-betrayal begin to fall away and we start to live in an authentic way. Gradually, the True Self arises in us and we are reborn into a different life.

The True Self understands the law of attraction and uses it on a daily basis. It understands that it does not create in a vacuum, so it surrenders its expectations to support the common good. It adapts as necessary to the situation that presents itself, yet it never betrays itself or its purpose. On the big issues it remains committed, focused and clear.

The Law of Attraction works well for those who have healed their wounds and nurtured their gifts. It does not work for those who are unconsciously driven by their wounds and in denial of their gifts.

So I have to keep reminding my students to slow down and do their emotional healing work.

Once you have done the work, attraction will happen by itself. You won't have to try to make it happen.

So "Stop pretending to be Ghandi or Martin Luther King," I tell them. "Get back in the sauce. You are still uncooked meatballs!"

We don't realize that Ghandi and King were meatballs too and they had to stay in the sauce until they were cooked. They had to stay on low, persistent heat until God smelled the aroma and knew they were ready.

The same is true for you and me. We all have an assignment

here and we will begin doing it when we are ready. If we try to do the work before we are ready, we will create such a mess that we may lose our desire to show up for the assignment we have.

So, please, leave the Law of Attraction alone until you know who you are and what you want. Until then, do nothing. Just stay in the sauce. Otherwise you will turn the Law of Attraction into the Law of Detraction and it won't feel very good to you.

Don't detract from yourself by seeking to attract something you don't think you have. Indeed, don't do any math at all. Don't seek to add on because there is nothing lacking. And if you don't add on, you won't have to subtract it later on when you realize you don't need it.

Addition and subtraction are part and parcel of the dualistic drama of life. Don't waste your time with the drama of ups and downs, pluses and minuses. Get back in the sauce and cook for a while.

When you are a cooked meatball, you will no longer try to get something that you don't need and you won't have to give it back once you get it. You save yourself a lot of heartache and a lot of guilt. When you don't create a mess, you don't have to clean it up.

Here are some common misunderstandings to avoid.

Misunderstanding #1: I Can Create What I Want.

Ultimately true. Wrong for right now. Right now you will create what you don't want and don't need. If you could create what you really want right now you would be doing it. So if you aren't doing it, admit temporary defeat and get back in the sauce. You aren't cooked enough yet.

Misunderstanding #2: I Know What I Want.

Think again. Most people haven't got the slightest idea what they want. They have just borrowed ideas from their parents and other authority figures. It works better to get clear on what you don't want and see what's left over. On the other hand, if you know what you want, better make it your top priority.

Misunderstanding #3: I am Here to Help Others.

Yes, that's true. But first you need to help yourself and heal your own wounds. Until you do that you won't be very helpful to others.

Misunderstanding #4: I Can have All the Money I want.

Well, maybe. Some people are good at business and finance. Some are not. Even those who are good at it aren't necessarily happy. If you have trouble making ends meet, take the next step and get a job. Most people don't win the lottery or inherit a fortune.

Misunderstanding #5: I can have the Perfect Relationship

If you are being sarcastic here, then I agree with you. It will be the "perfect" relationship to push your buttons and make you aware of all the healing you still need to do. By the way, have you ever noticed that the words "relationship" and "rocketship" have similar endings. I don't believe that's a coincidence!

Anyway, folks, it's time to wake up about this Law of Attraction. If you don't know who you are or what you want, how are you going to attract right livelihood or right relationship?

I know you are going to hate this, but I have to tell you the truth. I have met only four or five people who really know who they are and what they want. Of course, those four or five have no trouble attracting what they want or expressing who they are in this life.

But that's only four or five people and they are not necessarily the ones who are talking about the Law of Attraction. Most of the people I know are beating themselves up with the Law of Attraction That is why I don't mention it to my students until they are ready.

There are a lot of generals who will send the troops out to fight even though they are outnumbered and outgunned by the enemy. It doesn't hurt them much. They are watching the war from their skybox and are in no imminent danger.

Well, I just can't be that kind of general. I don't want to send a man or woman out into the trenches before s/he knows what s/he is doing and has a chance to succeed. So I spend a lot of time on preparation and training.

Many of our Mastery students have been in training for two to three years and they are just beginning to understand and to cooperate with the Law of Manifestation. In order to learn this Law, they had to slow down. They had to transform from being the hare to being the turtle. They had to get off the rocketship and put some roots in the ground.

They had to learn to love themselves, moment to moment. They had to keep repeating the question "Am I loving myself right now?" as a mantra to help them remember.

This is not pie-in-the-sky spirituality. It's chop wood, carry water. Stop spinning out and get grounded. Slow down. Move the energy out of your head and into your heart. Breathe. Practice awareness.

People want to leave the nest before they are ready. Fledging birds need to test their wings and take short trips between neighboring trees. Then, when their wings are strong and they feel confident, they can blast off into the sky and nothing will hold them back!

If you aren't ready, don't leave the nest. Stay and learn the skills you need to succeed. Practice and prepare. A great carpenter can do wonders with a few simple hand tools, but a novice will make a mess even with the most sophisticated tools.

If you are just learning to drive, please refrain from buying a Rolls Royce from the estate of the Bhagwan. Otherwise, it will take you less than an hour to total that car! Instead, buy a junker and practice driving it. Then you can work your way up to a better car.

Some parents buy their kids the best musical instruments as soon as they submit to their first music lesson. Three months later, the music store buys them back for half price. You would think that by now they would be choosing the rental program!

Well, what can you do? As much as you would like to prevent people from battering their heads against the proverbial wall, you can't force them to stop until they are ready. Sometimes it's a rather bloody affair and it's hard to watch.

As an antidote—to try to inculcate some sense into those insecure and unstable minds—I have decided to make huge billboards and to place them in all the major cities in the world. On each billboard will be a large pot with steam coming out.

And underneath the pot there will be this question "Are you an Uncooked Meatball?" along with a toll free number. I expect that many people will call that number asking why I have placed such a strange add on the billboard in their city. So I will ask my friend Hans to explain to them The Law of Detraction.

I can see it now: light bulbs will go off in their minds and they will drop instantly into their hearts. Suddenly, they will understand why nothing they do works and why Murphy is continually elected president and chairman of the board.

Of course, if Hans has his way, we will make a movie. And before long, we will be forced to go public. Meatballs and sauce will be everywhere. We will have more signs than Toyota! We might even take out an add during halftime of the Superbowl. I can see it now, can't you? Big steaming pot with thick rich sauce and a deep voice asking, *"Are you an uncooked meatball? Is the Law of Detraction running your life?"*

Now, I don't want to be too disrespectful to the Law of Attraction people because many of my friends are in that movie (which perhaps, not surprising to you, I have yet to see!). I know that sometimes you can't make a point unless you water the message down. But being Italian, I have to tell you it hurts when someone puts water in the sauce.

We have discussed this at length in our Spiritual Mastery Community and come to the conclusion that "Spirituality Lite" is better than "No Spirituality at all."

So when all of your friends come over raving about The Law of Attraction, just smile at them and don't let on that you read this chapter. And, most importantly, don't admit that you had that long heart to heart conversation over the telephone with Hans!

EARNING YOUR PHL DEGREE

Many of our Mastery students are overachievers. They have classical Spiritual Law Number Seven "Got to prove myself to you" syndrome. Some have already earned seven or eight PhDs and they really want two or three more. So there has been a great deal of demand for a Doctorate degree program. To satisfy this need, I set up several options for overachievers.

The first is the regular PhD program. This degree stands for People helping Ducks. It is based on the idea that "If it looks like a duck, if it quacks like a duck, then it must be a duck." At first, I offered to give any graduate of the Mastery Program a PhD degree, but this met with a lot of resistance.

"We need to do extra work if we are to earn this degree," they told me. So I reluctantly agreed and told them that they would have to go down to the lake every morning and clean up after the ducks. They weren't too crazy about this idea, but they did it anyway, so I had to go out and get some diplomas printed.

Then, some of these overachievers came to me and said, "Now that we have a PhD, isn't there some other kind of degree that we can get?" So I thought about it and then I told them, "Well you could get a PhL degree."

"What's that?" they asked, barely disguising their mounting excitement.

"That stands for People helping Llamas," I told them cracking a little bit of a smile.

Surprisingly, they liked this idea. "Of course," I told them, "you will have to do extra work to earn this degree. You will have to go out to the pasture and clean up after the Llama's."

Well, now they could no longer hold back their excitement. They were literally jumping up and down and rubbing their hands together. They couldn't wait to get to work.

Anyway, to make a long story short, they helped me come up with 24 additional doctoral degree programs that they could enroll in after they completed the PhL program. Indeed, there was one program for each letter of the alphabet. There was a PhA program (People helping Avacados), a PhB program (People helping Butterflies), a PhC program (People Helping Chipmunks), and so forth.

Raimonda Receiving her Ph.L Degree Photo: Bill Bogan

Amazingly, the more degrees we came up with, the more people started applying to the Mastery Program. It got to the point where I just had to say "Enough!" I had to put a ceiling on the degree thing because it was taking us completely off track.

You see it's really hard to stay grounded when you keep looking for the ceiling without finding it. And I knew that there would be a lot of people tripping over their own feet if we didn't bring their attention back to the ground.

So I told everyone, "It doesn't matter how many degrees you get you still have to cook for at least two years in the sauce and the number of degrees you get doesn't give you any status in the program."

And that seemed to do it. Now, you can get no degrees or 26 degrees. It's totally up to you. If you like to work hard and clean up doo-doo, we have plenty for you to do. If you don't, you will save yourself (and us!) a lot of trouble.

CONNECTING WITH THE FEMININE SPIRIT

The problem with growing up in our left-brain-driven, achievement-oriented world is that no one feels valuable unless s/he is *doing* something. So it's do, do, do! Everyone has two or three jobs and six or seven hobbies. Even the kids go from karate to soccer, to yoga, to scouts, to SAT preparation class, to Junior Achievement. And on it goes. We have achievementitis!

That creates two types of people: the kind that buy the farm and jump through all of the hoops to win your approval, and the kind that get overwhelmed and drop out.

Generally speaking — and there are exceptions to the rule — the baby boomers dropped out early in their lives and then they got very serious. They seem to have made the transition from "flower child" to workaholic in about five to ten years. Both parents went to work and were absent from the home. To make up for their guilt they bought their kids expensive computers and other electronic toys. Gradually, these kids began to zone out.

Even those kids who dutifully swallowed their parent's achievement agendas—speeding from one activity to the next—began to rebel. They became anxious and had trouble sleeping. Some of them started to pop pills.

Now, many of these kids are on drugs just like their parents were in the sixties. Only now the drugs are more dangerous and the kids are stuck in a variety of depressing black holes that they can't seem to climb out of. Some are completely dysfunctional. They don't know how to think, how to go to school, how to hold a job. In some cases, it appears that they don't even remember how to brush their teeth or tie their shoes. They are still dependent on their parents who—perfect enablers that they are—keep on paying their rent and utility bills for fear that if they don't their kids will be homeless.

So we now have a crazy world with two types of people in it—people who do, do, do—and people who don't, don't, don't. Unfortunately, it is a predictable world in which the generations are polarized and each group slips deeper and deeper into its own destructive, solipsistic cycle. The fact that one group doesn't understand the other makes it hard for parents to rescue their children, no matter how hard they try.

We have to use challenging tactics to interrupt these destructive cycles. We just have to take the overachievers out of the classroom and put them into the marinara sauce. And we have to take the underachievers away from their computers and television sets and put them into boot camp, where attendance is mandatory and no excuses are permitted.

In the Mastery Program, we get both types of people. One says, "Can I please, please, please?" The other says, "No, I can't, can't, can't." To the first I say, "Of course you can but first get in the sauce." To the other I say, "I will teach you how to chop the onions. We need plenty of them in the sauce. You may cry a few tears while you chop, but tears make the sauce taste great. You don't even have to use salt."

Our formula is a simple, but elegant one. Group A (overachievers) need to slow down. Group B (underachievers) need to get a job.

A skilled mentor in the Mastery program just finds which way people are driving and asks them to "slow down" or "turn around." To the achievers we say, "There's nothing to get. You don't need your 402nd PhD. Just go over and feed the Llamas and give them some love too. Let your heart open up and, if you insist on being busy, be a busy be be, bee." To the underachievers we say, "After you finish making the beds, you can show up for that introductory physics class. If you need remedial math first, be our guest. Wherever you are, we have a class for you. So get moving and keep moving. There's plenty here to do, do, do."

It's all about balance, is it not? We are here to balance the Divine Father energy (Doing). with the Divine Mother energy (Being). In fact, we want our doing to come out of our being. That way whatever we do is done with heart.

Our world has too much of the Father, and not enough of the

Mother. We have too much head, and not enough heart, too much Logos and not enough Eros.

To act without a passion for what we are doing leads to self-betrayal. That is why we must connect with the heart and find our passion. If we don't, what we do will not satisfy.

We live in a world that is imbalanced. The individual/collective beliefs that support that imbalance are simple ones.

1. I must do something (even if I don't want to do it).

We must learn to question this belief. Often it is better to do nothing than to do something out of anxiety, boredom. or the anticipated criticism of the authority figures in our lives.

2. If I don't do something, I will starve and become a bag lady.

Not doing is undertaken not as a permanent solution, but as a break from doing what we know is not working. It is a time to center, to observe, to get perspective, to receive guidance or inspiration. In other words, it is a way of bringing in the Divine Mother energy when we really need it.

While the "bag lady" is not the highest expression of the Mother energy—and we could find another more nurturing expression—at least we got her sex right. We know it is the Mother that we need.

3. Doing more is better than doing less.

This is true only if what you are doing is working and is in harmony with your life. If it is not working or in harmony, doing less is better.

If we question these erroneous beliefs and assumptions, we can begin to bring balance into our lives. We can slow down, connect to our hearts, and begin to do things that we really care about and can be committed to. That way we will learn to create enthusiastically and responsibly. We won't betray ourselves. We won't procrastinate or make promises we can't keep.

LIVING IN BALANCE

When we learn to bring the feminine energy in and connect with our hearts, we bring balance to our psyche and to our lives. We don't do as much as we used to do, but what we do is more effective and harmonious. Because we are connected from the inside out, our thoughts, feelings and actions are more congruent and we achieve better results.

Because we are shooting closer to the bull's eye, we don't have to keep as many arrows in our quiver. We save time and money. We don't have to work so hard to compensate for our lack of skillfulness.

When the Father energy and the Mother energy are joined together, things flow out easily and without great effort. Because we have learned to be patient, we waste less energy. We act when it is time to act, even if it's on a moment's notice. We learn to seize the moment and to pick the fruit when it's ripe.

The Father energy — being more balanced — loses its aberrant, overbearing "make it happen" tone and quality. It softens and bides its time. It rests in the Mother until it is time for it to act. And when that time comes, it does not hesitate. It leaps forth with energy, conviction and self-confidence. Is it any wonder that it hits the mark?

We work with the Mother energy not to become passive or helpless, but to rest, to center, to find inner strength and direction. These capabilities are necessary if we are to be happy in our hearts and effective in the world.

To be joyful, we must find our joy and learn to trust it. Divine mother makes that possible by inviting us into her sanctuary. There we learn to become still, to accept ourselves and receive her unconditional love. It is our incubation chamber.

The chick will be born when the chick is ready. Until then, let it remain in the shell. Let it have the steady heat of the Mother's acceptance and love. Let it become strong and confident. Then it can crash through the shell and be born into the world.

Many of the students in our Mastery program are impatient. They do not want to stay in the womb energy. They do not trust it. They have not learned how to receive Mother's love. They want to leave the womb before they are ready. If they do, they will abort or suffer necessary injury and trauma.

A half cooked meatball has a hard time being successful in this world. He is anxious and insecure. He scares people away. And those who are brave enough to take a bite usually have to spit it out right away. That doesn't do much for his confidence.

The hardest thing I have to do as a Spiritual mentor and guide is to keep people in the sauce until they are fully cooked. They keep jumping out of the sauce saying, "I'm ready now, aren't I?" And I have to keep telling them, "You're getting there, but you still have a ways to go."

I usually know when someone is cooked because I can smell the aroma. And then I have a different challenge with some of my people. I tell them, "You're ready now. Time to get out of the sauce and move your legs. You are ready to serve." And they look at me like I just told them their mother had died. "Do I have to get out of the sauce? Can't I stay in a little longer? I don't want to go out on the road. I want to stay in this nice little spiritual community where I know I am safe."

"No," I tell them. "If you stay, you will get overcooked. And that won't be good for you or for anyone else. It's time for you to step into your life purpose. You are ready to share your light and your love with others."

At first, they go forth from the nest a little tentatively. They really aren't sure that they are ready. But they learn to take small steps and to test their wings. And the universe supports them. Before long, they are flying high and doing the most amazing maneuvers.

I now know how a Momma hawk must feel when the little hawks leave the nest. As she looks out into the sky, she sees them circling confidently overhead. And she knows that her job is done.

The little hawks have gown and come into their power. Their childhood is over. Their apprenticeship is complete.

PART 9

A Healed World

We were told you would come
to heal your pain, to open your heart
to the power of love, to become
the light in the wilderness.

Healing Our Collective Wound

Anyone who has been through our Spiritual Mastery Program will tell you "If I can heal, you can heal. It simply requires your willingness."

Generally we are not willing until the pain becomes unbearable. Then and only then do we ask for help. The same dynamics seem to apply to the collective healing process.

Some groups of people have a low pain threshold and begin their healing journey early on. They establish communities where love abides and does its work. They nurture themselves and their environment. They come back into harmony with the earth.

Other groups have a high pain threshold. They go to war and brutalize each other and the earth. They live and die by the sword. This has occurred throughout human history. So what is different now?

What is different is that the brutality is now planetary-wide. No longer will peaceful groups be able to live out their lives apart from the maddening crowd. There is now one destiny for all the peoples — indeed all the creatures — of planet Earth.

We can no longer live in isolation. We can no longer live in denial of our pain, nor can we live with those who are in denial. We must reach out and offer to help.

Whenever we witness injustice or brutality, we can say to those who are suffering: "If you are in pain we can help. We have made the journey from fear to love. We can show you the way through the dark tunnel of your pain."

Not all whom we address will reach out and take our hand. But some of them will. And those are the ones that we are here to help.

Right now, our numbers are few, but more will come. More people will hit their pain threshold and come to us for healing and empowerment. We are here to serve them.

As more of us heal our wounds and begin to offer our gifts, our numbers will grow and we will be able to facilitate healing for larger numbers of people on the planet.

Some time ago, there was a movie called *Field of Dreams.* In it a man received a vision from God to build a baseball field in the middle of nowhere. Everyone thought he was crazy. But he was told by God: "If you build it they will come." And they did.

For three years now, we have been building a powerful community of people who are devoted to a deep emotional healing process. Those who have come to join us have been courageous. It has not been easy for them to face their fears and bring love to their wounds. But they have done this.

And now their lives are transformed. Now, they are ready to share their healing with you.

We are building this community because we were told that you would come. We were told that there would come a time in your life when you would know that you could not shift the pain by yourself. And you would reach out to us.

We came here for our own healing, but we stay here for yours. We know that when you are ready you will find us.

Three years ago, when I received the vision for this work, I was told that the Earth was in crisis and people would need a place where they could heal and connect with the high frequency energies of unconditional acceptance and love.

Before I received that vision, I thought that my work on Earth was done. I had written over thirty books and for thirty years I had held transformational workshops, retreats and conferences all over the world.

But I was wrong. My work was not done.

I was asked to do one more thing. I was asked to build this community. I knew that I could not do this by myself, so I put out a call to all of my readers. I told them, "If you are ready to move from your head to your heart, if you are ready to transform your life and be in service to our planet, join me now. We have a great work to do together."

The first wave of people came. Many were drawn by the energy, but only a few stayed. Only a few were truly committed. They became the nucleus of our community, the minion who would help me hold the work and extend it to others.

Then the second wave came from countries all over the globe. And so our international healing community was birthed and it continues to grow steadily.

People come and open their hearts to the power of love and bring it home with them. They become the light in the wilderness. They become the voice of love that speaks when fear rises.

Today, it is no longer possible for men and women of good

faith to sit on the sidelines while the human race goes down to its most ignominious defeat. Today, everyone who cares has to get into the game.

It doesn't matter if you don't know what your gift is or how to give it. If you volunteer, you will find out.

In case you wondered, our team has a very long bench with plenty of seats on it. Plus we have one of the best coaches in the business. If you come to one of our retreats, you will get to meet her!

If the stories in this book have made your heart sing, maybe your name is on one of those seats. If not, there is another team that needs you.

In the final analysis, it doesn't matter what team you join. Join whichever one speaks to your heart. But don't hold back. Don't procrastinate. Don't think that your healing and your gift don't matter.

They absolutely do matter!

Today, many lights are needed and many voices need to be lifted up. May yours be among them!

Namaste,

Paul Ferrini

Paul Ferrini is the author of over 30 books on love, healing and forgiveness. His unique blend of spirituality and psychology goes beyond self-help and recovery into the heart of healing. His conferences, retreats, and *Affinity Group Process* have helped thousands of people deepen their practice of forgiveness and open their hearts to the divine presence in themselves and others.

For more information on Paul's work, visit the web-site at *www.paulferrini.com*. The website has many excerpts from Paul Ferrini's books, as well as information on his workshops and retreats. Be sure to request Paul's free email newsletter, as well as a free catalog of his books and audio products. You can also email: info@**heartwayspress.com** or write to **Heartways Press, 9 Phillips Steet, Greenfield, MA 01301.**

Explore the Other Spiritual Mastery Books

If you like this book, you may want to read the other books in the series. They are briefly described below.

The first book— *The Laws of Love*—contains ten essential spiritual principles that we need to master in order to heal and step into our life purpose.

The second book— *The Power of Love*—contains ten spiritual practices that help us connect with our Core Self, our Source, and the gift that we are here to give.

The third book— *The Presence of Love*—helps us understand the masculine/feminine aspects of the Divine and shows us how to embody the unconditional love that will heal us and our planet.

The fourth book— *Love is My Gospel*—looks at the life and teachings of one spiritual master (Jesus) as an example of what is possible for us.

The fifth book — *Real Happiness* –shows us how to heal our wounds at depth and awaken the joy that is our birthright.

The book you are reading— *Embracing Our True Self*—the sixth book in the Mastery series—describes the three stages in the process of healing and transformation and offers case histories of people who have transformed their lives in our community.

Paul Ferrini's *Course in Spiritual Mastery*

Part Six: Embracing Our True Self
A New Paradigm Approach to Healing Our Wounds, Finding Our Gifts, and Fulfilling Our Spiritual Purpose
192 pages $13.95
ISBN # 978-1-879159-69-3

Part Five: Real Happiness
A Roadmap for Healing Our Pain and Awakening the Joy That Is Our Birthright
160 pages $12.95
ISBN # 978-1-879159-68-6

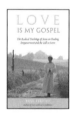

Part Four: Love is My Gospel
The Radical Teachings of Jesus on Healing, Empowerment and the Call to Serve
128 pages $12.95
ISBN # 1-879159-67-8

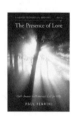

Part Three: The Presence of Love
God's Answer to Humanity's Call for Help
160 pages $12.95
ISBN # 1-879159-62-7

Part Two: The Power of Love
10 Spiritual Practices that Can Transform Your Life
168 pages $12.95
ISBN # 1-879159-61-9

Part One: The Laws of Love
A Guide to Living in Harmony
with Universal Spiritual Truth
144 pages $12.95
ISBN # 1-879159-60-0

Paul's In-depth Presentation of the Laws of Love on 9 CDs

THE LAWS OF LOVE
Part One (5 CDs) ISBN # 1-879159-58-9 $49.00
Part Two (4 CDs) ISBN # 1-879159-59-7 $39.00

These are only a few of the many titles available.
To order or receive a free catalog of Paul Ferrini's Books and
Audio products, contact: Heartways Press 9 Phillips Street,
Greenfield, MA 01301   413-774-9474
Toll free: 1-888-HARTWAY
email: info@heartwayspress.com

You may also purchase these products on-line
by visiting our website
www.Paul Ferrini.com